green architecture for the future

Louisiana Museum of Modern Art
Frontiers of Architecture II

Curator Kjeld Kjeldsen
Assistant curator Mette Marie Kallehauge
Consultant Peter Andreas Sattrup
Exhibition coordinator Arne Schmidt-Petersen
Architect, Graphic designer Steen Heide
Art handler Ulrik Staal Dinesen
Graphic designer Bente Stensen Christensen
Exhibition architect Mads Kjædegaard
Architects Gudrun Krabbe, Jens Kamp and
Anders Christiansen
Stud.art Jeppe Priess Gersbøll

Laboratories I and II, City
Curators:
Foster + Partners
Ecosistema Urbano

Climate
Curators:
Climate Engineering Transsolar/ Mathias Schuler,
Monika Lauster
Ockert und Partner/ Frank Ockert
Behnisch Architekten

Laboratory III, Climate
Curator: Philippe Rahm

Laboratory IV, Metabolism
Curator: R&Sie(n)

Installations in Louisiana Park
United_Bottle Group UBG
Nicola Basic
3XN/GXN

Realdania
Sponsor of architectural exhibitions at Louisiana

DONG energy   **Sponsor for Louisiana Museum of Modern Art 2009**

The City

Climate

Metabolism

Foreword

Climate zones. Climate shock. Minister for the Climate. Climate Summit, Copenhagen. You name it...

The focus on the climate and all things related – and that's quite a mouthful – really is a focus. And thus also a focus on all things related. And that's quite a mouthful too, for messages of salvation and perdition are crowding in from all conceivable directions – from the pessimists' apocalyptic warnings of the imminent end of the world to the irrepressible optimists' faith in technology. The former can lead to defeatism and political stalling or corner-cutting in democratic societies that may suddenly find themselves forced in certain directions by the *fait accompli* of the climate threat; the latter – despite all inventiveness – can lead to a backlash, since technological advances may be hitched to more than one bandwagon, for example the one that leads to the perpetuation of the same old habits of consumption, now just 'new and improved'.

How are we to relate to this spectrum, where Judgement Day and miracle are like two sides of the same coin? Is there a way of thinking – a commonsense pragmatism – that can carry us through, or has the whole human perspective hit a brick wall? Does nature have rights, or only us? Does the poor part of the world have the right to SUVs – or is that only us too? And what am I to do? And what is the architect to do?

It isn't the privilege or duty of any art museum, including the Louisiana, to provide answers and point out solutions to this. All the same, in the Louisiana's activities over the past 50 years there certainly has been a clear strand that makes us participants in this debate. The purpose of the museum is to gather together images of the times – past, present and future – such that these images enhance our true knowledge of and sensitivity to the options offered, in this case by architecture, in our precarious situation.

So it isn't the crisis as such that provides the central metaphor for the Louisiana's exhibition. After all, the future of architecture is green! No, once again it's the presentation of what is actually happening in the world right now that takes centre stage. And that presentation is driven by the same commitment that drives all our architectural exhibitions, the desire not only to trace out the aesthetic lines in the development of architecture, but also to reveal the relationships between architecture and society. That is what interests us at the Louisiana. And that is why we show exhibitions about architecture – as a vital supplement to exhibitions of and about visual art.

Green Architecture for the Future is the second exhibition in the series *Frontiers of Architecture*. The series began in 2007 with the presentation of the Sri Lankan-English engineer Cecil Balmond under the title *The Hidden Order*. While that exhibition was about the mathematical-philosophical parameters for the realization of new architecture, the present exhibition has more to do with 'the visible disorder' – that is, the vast field marked out by discussions of sustainability, with its wide range of challenges.

Obviously the exhibition has a sense of obligation in the face of all the observations that can be stacked up into ominous towers of despair over the state of the planet; but the fundamental tone of the exhibition is not pessimistic. The museum, the Louisiana, is an institution that is ultimately a product of the Enlightenment, and duly considers it crucial to present the energy or vitality that drives many responsible architects as they grapple with the current situation. We give the floor – and the walls and the spaces – to architects and architectural philosophers who are trying to view the architecture of the future as living machines, cities as new and different structures, buildings as 'intelligent', so that they are not only self-sufficient but also make positive contributions to their surroundings, create biological diversity, produce cleaner air and discharge water that is cleaner than when it came into the building.

In this context architecture can be understood as an organism with a lifetime and a metabolism whose material is regularly replaced, broken down and re-emerges as new and better materials. Maybe the skyscraper of tomorrow will have moss-clad facades that help us to purify the city air, integrated solar-powered heating, trees and bushes that produce energy and create microclimates and biodiversity for the benefit of animals and birds, and colours that change with the seasons.

Conceiving buildings as systems of diversified, living components means that different materials with different lifetimes can be replaced independently of one another without a radical renovation of the whole building. This enables the architect to design the building so that it not only meets the needs we have for space today, but so that future generations will also have the opportunity to reprogramme the building, functionally as well as technically. Maybe in fifteen years' time there will new sustainable materials that can optimize the various subcomponents of the building over time – and the building will slowly be adapted – formally as well as functionally – to technological advances. The architects of industrialism knew that form follows function – today maybe we should say that form must follow evolution.

There are many maybes. But instead of reading this little word 'maybe' in the spirit of scepticism over wild imaginings, the exhibition documents how this word 'maybe' packs a conceptual punch which in turn grows out of a willingness to transform our competencies. The architects who are today daring to think differently are certainly suffering from no paralysis of the will. On the contrary, nothing is too great, nothing too small, to be drawn into the orbit of care for the future – nature, the city, the materials, social organization and even our clothes and shoes: the list is endless.

In this area, architecture has for a while rediscovered its status as an applied art, and there are two things that suggest that this maybe (!) carries it beyond the past century's aesthetic discussions of architecture: first, that our concept of aesthetics is maybe (!) too limited; secondly, that the most interesting architecture is the kind that stays out on the frontiers of architecture, which is thus not a line in the sand, but an area, a field, a zone.

The exhibition *Green Architecture for the Future* situates itself in this zone, where architecture is intersected and criss-crossed by science, politics, ethics and social vision.Putting together such a complex exhibition with such a great variety of projects as *Green Architecture for the Future* – and presenting this vast subject in general – requires more knowledge than any individual can muster. It is a collective process involving a wide range of people with their fields of expertise, people we would therefore like to thank for their invaluable contributions – their helpfulness, advice, guidance and commitment.

The pivotal feature of the exhibition is four laboratories to which the Louisiana has invited four international architects. They were chosen on the basis of their very different and not least innovative approaches to the concept of sustainable architecture. We are grateful that they have accepted the invitation with enthusiasm – so our great and heartfelt gratitude to Jose Luis Vallejo and Belinda Tato/ Ecosistema Urbano; to Foster + Partners, especially Katy Harris; to François Roche and R&Sie(n); and to Philippe Rahm.

The various sections of the exhibition in the large field that makes up sustainable theory and practice have been mounted in collaboration with people who have each in their own way contributed material and knowledge. We owe a great debt of thanks to the climate engineers Transsolar, especially Monika Lauster, and to the designer and graphic designer Frank Ockert and Behnisch Architects, for making their large body of material available and for their design contributions to the presentation of Transsolar's scientific and theoretical thinking.

In this connection we would also like to thank Heiko Wassbach from Sauerbruch Hutton for his commitment and help, and Copijn for technical sponsorship.

Thanks also to Michael Braungart Chemistry Design, William McDonough + Partners and in particular to the architect Mark Rylander for insight and assistance in the presentation of one of the most important theories of modern sustainable development, Cradle to Cradle.

We thank 3XN, GXN and Kasper Guldager Jørgensen for their enthusiasm and ideas – and for the great effort they have devoted to the creation of the pavilion with the new intelligent materials in the Louisiana Park. Without GXN's expert insight and wide network this project would not have seen the light of day.

We thank our project partners: 3XN, architects and project management; COWI, engineering and light design; Stage One Freeform Composites, production and installation; BASF, the chemical company, phase changing materials; Micronal PCM, cimate control, phase changing materials; Ashland Inc., producer of bioresin; TransFurans Chemicals, producer of bioresin; Amorim Cork Composites, producer of cork; Libeco-Lagae, producer of natural fibers; ENKEV Natural Fibres, producer of natural fibers; Flex Cell, producer of flexible photo voltaic; Phillips, producer of led light; Scenetek, intallation of eletrical components; Noliac Motion, producer of piezoelectric materials; Optima Projects Limited, composite counseling; NetComposites Ldt, network within composites; Danish Technological Institute, selfcleaning counseling; Risø National Laboratory DTU, composite testing.

For expertise and inspiring discussions we would like to send our thanks to the architects Tanja Jordan and Kirsten Birk, art historian Elisabeth Bodin as well as Signe Kongebro from the Henning Larsen architectural office.

And our thanks to the architect Dorthe Mandrup for the interest she has shown and the good advice she has provided.

Our particular gratitude must go to Mette Marie Kallehauge, who as co-curator of the exhibition participated in the formulation of the idea and the final concept, and in the gathering and selection of the large body of material. Great thanks also to the architect and PhD student Peter Andreas Sattrup, on whose great expertise in sustainability we have drawn throughout the process.

Last but not least, thanks to all the artists and architects who have contributed to the exhibition: 3XN/ Will Alsop Architects/ Nicola Basic/ Patrick Blanc/ Behnisch Architekten/ COBE/ Copijn/ ENTASIS/ Roland Castro/ Frederic Druot/ GrAT/ Jaime Lerner/ Ken Yeang/ Lacaton & Vassal/ John Mardaljevic/ Mario Cucinella Architects/ METI School Project, Anna Heringer & Eike Roswag/ Mette Lange/ Michel Desvigne/ MVRDV/ Shrinking Cities, Philipp Oswalt/ PTW Architects/ Richard Rogers/ Sarah Wigglesworth/ Sauerbruch Hutton/ Shigeru Ban/ Stefano Boeri Studio/ Studio Monte Rosa, Professor Andrea Deplazes, ETH/ Tanja Jordan/ Transsolar, Matthias Schuler/ United_ Bottle Group UBG/ An Te Liu/ Ton Matton. Also, thanks to SEACEX, the Spanish Cultural Institute, for support to Ecosistema Urbano.

Finally, our thanks to the exhibition coordinator Arne Schmidt-Petersen, the architect and graphic designer Steen Heide, the art handler Ulrik Staal Dinesen, the exhibition architect Mads Kjædegaard, the architect Gudrun Krabbe and the graphic designer Bente Steensen. And to the trainees Jens Kamp, Anders Christiansen and Jeppe Priess Gersbøll.

Realdania, the Louisiana's sponsor for architecture exhibitions, has on this occasion too ensured that the exhibition could become a reality – as Chapter Two of the series *Frontiers of Architecture*.

Kjeld Kjeldsen & Poul Erik Tøjner

THE CITY

LAB I

What if...? – Cities

The development of the cities throughout the twentieth century has led to uncertainties about the future. In recent decades, new urban fragments have appeared – fragments that are not properly part of the city, but 'non-places' – and these places influence the design of the cities of the future for subsequent generations.

There is a different way of intervening in the cities: by optimizing, diversifying and regenerating urban space without consuming unnecessary resources, unnecessary amounts of money and without generating unnecessary waste. Interventions that can sow the seeds of regeneration and actively involve the resident of the city in their urban space.

What does sustainability mean to you? What if the architects had the same interests as the public? What if we could change the cities through creativity? What if everyone could take part in this transformation process? What if a small change could lead to big reactions? What if you could contribute with your own ideas at the Louisiana?

Ecosistema Urbano believes that cities are both part of the problem and part of the potential for the future. Urban life will not be revitalized by architecture alone, but by focusing on solutions that consider all the aspects of the city; social networks, environmental and physical components of flourishing, inhabitable urban communities.

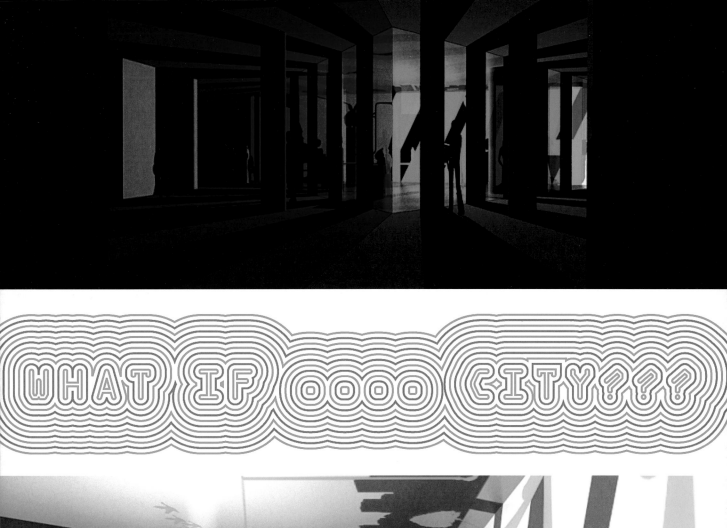

WHAT IF OOOO CITY???

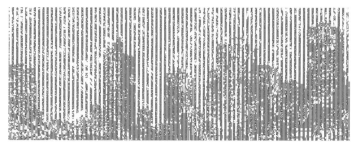

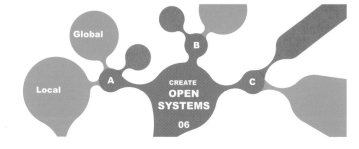

Ecosistema Urbano
Interview with José Luis Vallejo and Belinda Tato

By Peter Andreas Sattrup

PAS: When you put eco + system + urban together, you get a giant field of possible meanings. What is the background for your name, and how does it reflect your work?
BT: We wanted a name that was open-ended and had a message. We knew that for a long time there would only be the two of us, but the name had to get others than ourselves to identify with it and join in a collective venture. It's important to us that the name has a message, that it sets an agenda. But several people have pointed out that it also leaves us great scope: we can concentrate the focus on ecosistema or urbano as required.

What is the main thrust of your work? Do you have a special focus right now?
JLV: We're strongly focused on public space. We're interested in the social aspects of architecture, and when you consider what it is that makes a city, then what happens between the buildings is more important to us than what happens inside them. That's a point that has been forgotten for a long time. Architects mainly think of buildings as objects, and we aren't trained to understand public space in a particularly sophisticated way. It's simply where the building ends. There's a tendency to see it as a room in a building that can be dealt with by furnishing it with a couple of benches and a few plants here and there. But public space is everywhere around us, and it's much more complex.

BT: We're also working to see the city as a whole system. There's a tendency to separate things into architecture and urban planning, where urban planning has been considered less cool and creative for a long time. Calling ourselves ecosistema urbano reminds us and others that the city should be a goal in itself – there's really a need to improve our cities. It's fine to build a good house, but if you can do something that improves the city, that's even better. When you read architectural journals you see thou-sands of examples of buildings, but very few articles about good urban neighbourhoods, about urban spaces or master plans.
JLV: I think, too, that architects have had a tendency to forget people and only concentrate on their own ideas. Often there aren't even people in the pictures you see of architecture. But architecture is for people, not just for architects. That's why we should really involve ourselves in people's opinions and needs.

Since you're moving away from a classic understanding of the architect as a designer of buildings and material things, what is it that you're designing? For example you've worked with TV as part of a project to create a public space in Madrid. What do you consider to be your material, and which media do you use?
JLV: We miss out on lots of possibilities if we only take an interest in dead materials, wood and stone. Looking at the city, it's people who are the raw material. There are plenty of levels: energy, waste ... working with the city isn't like working with dead material in an isolated laboratory. The city is in con-stant flux, constantly developing, and we have to keep our eyes open and adapt to what is happening out there. There's lots of material to work with. Mass media is a good example. Architecture doesn't need to be so static. Of course there are those who ask whether what we do is actually architecture, but I think we experience great openness and a certain positive uncertainty about what we do.

Now that you have projects in many parts of the world, what do you see as the most pressing issues? Are there any common denominators that can link the projects together, or do they always relate specifically to the local circumstances?
BT: I think our methodological approach links the projects together, but the problems we deal with are very different. Philadelphia for example is an

has been the worst possible places – old garbage dumps for example. There are plenty of places where architects can really make a difference.

Now I'm curious; what is really your deepest motivation? Is it philanthropy?
BT: Ha ha – Yes, I'm laughing, for of course we should be thinking about the fact that we're running a business. But when you get down to it, it's about responsibility. In a way architects aren't particularly important – we don't save anyone's lives with architecture. On the other hand we have a huge opportunity to make a difference. I like to think of it as creating a landscape for happiness. Through the homes, schools, libraries and the city we are creating we have a major influence on people's lives. It's a huge responsibility. I noticed a school class on its way to the Louisiana, and imagined that it must be a wonderful place to grow up here. In Madrid children are in constant danger of being run over, and that's extremely stressful. The surroundings we create affect our lives to an incredible extent. We must also think about the fact that the surroundings we create live much longer than we do. We've inherited both good and bad decisions from the time before us, and our own work is the legacy we pass on, for better or worse. In Spain an incredible amount has been built that isn't very good. Landscapes have been completely ruined. Once that's been done, it can't be changed.

JLV: But the issue of the city and public space is taking over the agenda now. That's clear in the USA, but the same tendency can be seen throughout most of the world.

I didn't ask just to tease, but also so I could ask another question: much of the debate on sustainable architecture is driven by thinking about resource management, efficiency, the reduction of energy consumption. This thinking is directly related to economics, but also to social sustainability and the issue of how we create good environments. Where do you stand in this debate?
JLV: These days there are quite a few certifications, where you can get a label to stick on your building: this building is energy-efficient, with 702 points. But it's more complex than that: you can put up a zero-energy building that has destroyed a neighbourhood, or does nothing for public space. If you destroy the cultural heritage and value of a place, it isn't sus-

American city and has problems that are very different from the ones we experience in Madrid. The urban density and the traffic structures are quite different. In some areas the way people think can be very much the same, while in others there's a world of difference. But thanks to the Internet you can work across those boundaries. It's easy to search for information, and it can be an advantage to come in from the outside and see the issues with fresh eyes. But there are certain common features. When you look at the totality there will always be something that isn't efficient enough, and that means that you have to work with things like mobility, energy, resources, water and waste. It's always the same factors.

JLV: The development of the western cities has been driven by a strong sense of individualism. We've been preoccupied with building beautiful places in the middle of the city and out along the coasts. Now we've come to the point where we have to stop and look at what it is we've built, and find out what we can do with the worst places. We've always chosen to enter the competitions where the starting-point

tainable in my view. Creating a living, healthy place to spend time in involves much more than energy reductions.

BT: The most important resource is people. We build for the happiness and wellbeing of people.

I can imagine that certain places, for example the run-down areas of Philadelphia, present some very grim situations. What do you do to forge contacts, to involve people and get them to feel they have a stake in your projects?

BT: That isn't so simple, but it's very necessary. The social situation in the disadvantaged neighbourhoods in Philadelphia is very difficult to understand with European eyes. But the challenge was much more social and economic problems than architectural problems. We thought that no matter how brilliant the architects who win the competition are, it'll be a failure if they aren't attentive to the social situation.

If people don't accept the project, will it be destroyed?

BT: Certainly. There are various possibilities. You can create something really smart and grandiose, and force out the people who live there – that is, you don't solve any problems – or you can work with people, get their advice, involve them in the big decisions, and make them proud of their neighbourhood. That is an economic operation. But that's why there have to be areas that cater for the social needs, so that people can see that the project can help make their lives better, and they don't see it is something aggressive that wants to move them out and alienate them. If they get that idea, they'll do anything to break it down.

JLV: I believe in projects that first and foremost start processes where people are involved. It may be that it doesn't look like much to begin with, that it can't be drawn as an impressive plan, the way architects love

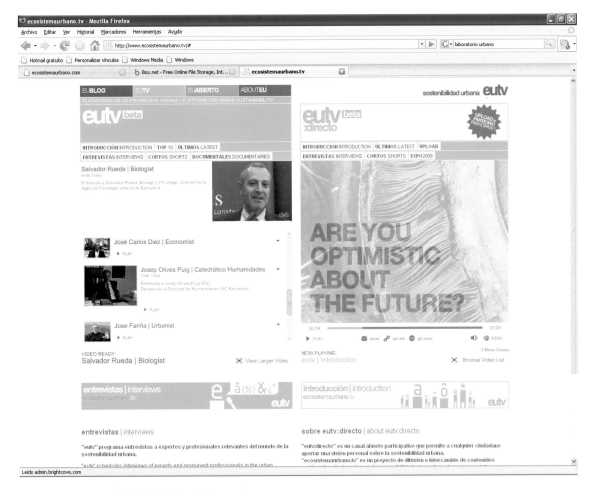

100 m

PLAZA LUNA - PLAYA LUNA
Service Area ✱✱✱✱✱

500 M3- ARENA   30 LITROS DE
8 DUCHAS   PINTURA
50 SOMBRILLAS   4 CARTELES
200 SILLAS   1 CHIRINGUITO

ESTE VERANO, CON 12.000 €,
LLEVAMOS LA PLAYA A MADRID.

✱✱✱✱✱✱✱✱✱✱✱✱

to do it. But I don't care – after all no one is ever going to be looking at it from the air! I'm more interested in creating life, creating connections. We're trying to increase the complexity. And the processes we set in motion will also change over time. We've been trained to follow linear processes – if only you do such-and-such, you'll get a good result. I don't believe in that. A project is always also a discussion, always up for negotiation and possible revision. It isn't just about implementing the first idea.

You talk about what you call "urban acupuncture" as your process and method?
JLV: Yes, actually that isn't our concept, it's a reference to Jaime Lerner, who showed how you can achieve an incredible amount with very small resources in Curitiba in Brazil; how you can start enormous improvements of the city with small steps, care and time.

"Urban acupuncture" sounds like a very gentle, almost humble approach. But what it you were given the opportunity to implement your ideas with no limits, anywhere in the world. You could solve the problems of a place, a city. Where would you start, where would you go with it?

JLV: I don't care for the idea of First-World architects going off to the Third World and solving their problems, if I can put it that way. It's worthless. Participation is the thing. The most successful collaborations are those where you build something together and the process helps to professionalize the participants.

BT: We pay attention to the small things. The competition among architects is fierce and you have to be inventive to find new directions, in purely professional terms. But through small things you can make great changes. It isn't a matter of being humble. Maybe we are doing very little, but we expect a great deal from it. And it's effective. Maybe we spend 10,000 Euros planting 20 trees, but they'll change a place completely. And the unofficial approach is quicker. If you have to go through the official systems you quickly spend several million, and it takes years – if it ever happens. We're faster, cheaper – and smarter!

We are seeing great migrations of people and cities growing up within just a few years. At the same time we have the challenges of climate change. There are great

challenges, and many people would think that the answer is master plans. Your approach seems very different?

BT: Grand plans can become grand failures if they aren't good enough. The grander, the bigger the failure. A small problem can have a big solution hidden within it. So master plans don't appeal as much to me as just dealing with a waste problem in a particular city. We want to be very close to reality.

Shrinking Cities

2002-2008
Büro Philipp Oswalt, Berlin

Since the onset of industrialization approximately two hundred years ago, populations, economies, levels of wealth, and cities in industrial countries have been growing virtually constantly, for the most part at a rapid pace. Growth seems to have become a matter of course. Modernity continues to be marked by a belief in processes of growth which forms the basis of its ideas and concepts for action, theories, laws, and practices.

However, this historical epoch is drawing to a close.

At the turn of the nineteenth century, two percent of a total world population of one billion lived in cities. It is estimated that by 2050, about seventy-five percent of a total global population of some 8.5 billion will live in cities. But not all cities are growing.

Between 1950 and 2000, more than 350 large cities experienced, at least temporarily, significant declines in population. In the 1990s, more than a quarter of the world's large cities shrank, and their number is continually increasing.

Just as expansion once did, shrinkage has fundamental repercussions which – through changes in approaches, models of action and practices – result in social reorientation.

For six years, the project *Shrinking Cities* studied the causes and effects of processes of urban shrinkage and sought new scope for development.

The exhibition Shrinking Cities is in three chapters, and begins with a scientific and artistic analysis of this global phenomenon, focusing on six case studies in developed industrial nations in North America, Europe, and Asia. In the second part of the exhibition, nine ideas are presented as approaches to concepts of action for shrinking cities. The third part of the exhibition provides forecasts that afford us a glimpse into the future.

The Future has Arrived - Architecture in a sustainable world shows parts of the first chapter, the analysis of the phenomenon of 'shrinking cities', and in addition to a global overview of the phenomenon and its causes, six urban regions in the old industrial countries of Europe, North

America, and Asia are presented as examples. Each of these case studies focuses on one of the typical causes of shrinkage: the 'Motor City' Detroit (USA) represents shrinkage due to processes of suburbanization; the former industrial region Manchester / Liverpool (UK) illustrates shrinkage due to de-industrialization; the seaport Hakodate (Japan) shrinkage due to demographic aging; and the textile region of Ivanovo (Russian Federation) exemplifies shrinkage due to post-socialist change. These international examples are seen alongside the region of Halle / Leipzig in Eastern and the Ruhr area in western Germany.

Population Movements 1998-2002

Finland

Baltics

Russian Federation

other Eastern European countries

Kazakhstan

Central and Western Europe

former Yugoslavia

Caucasia

Tajikistan

Turkey

Iran

Afghanistan

Korea (South)

Japan

Tunisia

Iraq

Middle East

China

Morroco

Algeria

India and Pakistan

Myanmar

Vietnam

Hongkong

Western Sahara

Thailand

Philippines

other African countries

Chad

Eritrea

South East Asia

Guinea

Sudan

Somalia

Sierra Leone

Central African Republic

Sri Lanka

Liberia

Congo

Uganda

Kenya

Indonesia

Gabon

Dem. Rep. of Congo

Tanzania

East Timor

Angola

Zambia

Australia and New Zeeland

Main routes

Flight (according to UNHCR)

Migration (according to OECD)

Tourism (according to WTO)

>10 000 000 persons/year

1 000 000–10 0000 000 persons/year

100 000–1 000 000 persons/year

10 000–100 000 persons/year

Regions of origin

Refugees

Migrants

Tourists

Sources/Kilder: ILO 2006 – Migration Information Source, 2006 – OECD, 2005 – Refugees International, 2006 – UNHCR, 2003 – WTO, 2005

DETROIT   2003   1995

HALLE/LEIPZIG   2003   2004

IVANOVO   2003   2003

MANCHESTER/LIVERPOOL 1989 2002

HAKODATE 2005 2006

RUHRGEBIET 1985 1999

Urban Voids
Philadelphia

Philadelphia, 2006
Ecosistema Urbano, Madrid

Urban acupuncture gives Philadelphia more breathing spaces

Spanish Ecosistema Urbano has created a project that makes Philadelphia greener and gives the residents of the city new ways of getting together.

The fundamental idea of Ecosistema Urbano's urban development project for Philadelphia is to create ecological corridors that criss-cross the city and get people to move in new ways. The corridors are created by means of 'urban acupuncture', which intervenes with energy-friendly transport and more breathing-spaces. The city already has an extensive system of bicycle paths and this will be expanded so it becomes even easier to promote the bicycle as the most appealing means of transport. At the same time Ecosistema Urbano proposes a new generation of ecological vehicles in the form of bicycle-taxis that can transport people in quick, environment-friendly ways into the centre.

A new activity centre where the city residents can meet is also part of the plan. The activity centre is to be built in light, inexpensive materials such that the individual sections can change function as required. The idea is to build the centre in stages so that the various parts will only be added when there is a specific need and it makes sense economically. On the whole the project focuses on ensuring that the new power centres – 'urban catalysts' – will turn the negative social development around in slum areas of the city. The project also works with alternative energy in the form of a water-purifying system and wind turbines.

Ecosistema Urbano's vision for Philadelphia is that the city must form a more cohesive whole. The citizens of Philadelphia are to be actively involved in the project, and the combination of ecological breathing-spaces and new meeting-places means that the city will be given both an environmental and a social lift.

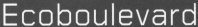

Ecoboulevard

Madrid, 2006
Ecosistema Urbano, Madrid

Recycling the non-city
The Eco Boulevard in Vallecas can be defined as an urban recycling operation consisting of the following elements: the erection of 'Air Tree' recycling pavilions along the course of an existing urbanization area, the concentration of the existing alignment trees, and the reduction and asymmetrical organization of wheeled traffic circulation, as well as superficial interventions to remove existing negative features of urbanization (gaps, fillings, paint, etc.) that deface the existing kerb development.

The Eco Boulevard Competition was organized with two objectives. One was the creation of venues that would generate and support social activity; and one was environmental – the bioclimatic adaptation of an outdoor space. Public spaces belong to everyone and they should support a variety of activities and events.

The best way of adapting a public space involves a dense aggregate of trees, a 'wood', but it takes 15 or 20 years for these to grow and be effective. So while such a 'wood' is the ulatimate aim, it has been necessary to take 'emergency' action with something that can operate as the trees will in the future.

Three pavilions or 'Air Trees' support multiple activities chosen by the users. Installed in the 'non-city' as temporary prostheses, they will remain in use only until the the lack of social activities and the climatic adaptation problem have been remedied. Once the necessary time has elapsed, these devices will be taken down, and their sites will remain as 'clearings' among the trees.

The Air Tree is a light structure that is self-sufficient in terms of energy and can be dismantled. It consumes only the energy it can produce with photovoltaic solar energy collection systems. The sale of excess energy to the power network generates a surplus in the annual balance sheet, which is reinvested in the maintenance of the structure itself.

Bosco Verticale

Milan, 2008
Stefano Boeri, Gianandra Barreca, Giovanni La
Varra, Milan

Bosco Verticale consists of two towers 110 og 76 metres tall, built in the centre of Milan. The walls of the towers are planted with more than 1000 trees, measuring up to 9 m, varies species of bushes and plants, and a 1300 m^2 planting on the outer walls. Altogether Bosco Verticale forms a forested surface of c. 10000m^2. By comparison the corresponding dwelling area is 50000m^2.

Manifesto for a vertical forest
01 BOSCO VERTICALE is a project for metropolitan reforestation.
02 BOSCO VERTICALE is a model of urban densification.
03 BOSCO VERTICALE is an anti-sprawl device that contributes to the control and reduction of urban expansion.
04 BOSCO VERTICALE can aid in the reduction of urban traffic congestion.
05 BOSCO VERTICALE creates a microclimate and filters small dust particles.
06 BOSCO VERTICALE is a system that optimizes, recovers and produces energy.
07 BOSCO VERTICALE increases biodiversity.
08 BOSCO VERTICALE is a landmark in an ever-changing landscape.
09 BOSCO VERTICALE is an urban sensor for spontaneous vegetable and animal re-colonization.
10 BOSCO VERTICALE increases urban ecological culture and awareness.

Urban Dystopi

Sustainable Dystopias is a research project that takes its point of departure in contemporary debate on the relationship between city and nature, and explores various ideas for reconciling the two. The project is divided into three main themes: plantings on vertical and horizontal surfaces in the city; innovative thinking about the interaction of animals and humans through a radical restructuring of the distribution of urban space, that is, the division into animal zones and human zones; and a technological vision that focuses on sustainable effectivization of the energy of the city by way of solar and wind power. In ultimate scenarios the three themes challenge our attitudes to the sustainability issue, taken here to its logical extremes, and thus calls for a critical awareness of the new perspectives.

1. Cultivating the city

The first evolutionary scenario concerns the possibility of adding agriculture and vegetation to our cityscapes, a possible dystopia to which is monocultural forms of agriculture reducing biodiversity and creating the risk of exterminating the hygienic separation between residential and agricultural uses that is so effective in the control of pests and diseases.

2. City of animals

The second scenario concerns the politics of re-naturalization and re-forestation within the built-up and compact areas of the city. Protected zones where people are banned would be open for the free growth of biodiversity, the cost may be an urban life that is no longer livable for people who, after abandoning these areas to other species, might end up escaping to theme parks outside the urban environment, amidst what remains of nature in today's world.

3. Nature technologized

The third and final visualization is linked to the widespread diffusion, also within the domestic sphere, of systems that reduce urban energy consumption with a new urban landscape made up of accumulators and surfaces that can capture solar and wind energy, as well as water collection systems, with the risk of these processes dominating the otherwise unpredictable aspects of human life and transforming the entire built-up world into a place of totalitarian control.

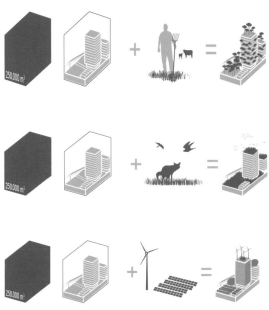

Grand Paris

Grand Paris, 2008

Paris is a fried egg

Any French president with respect for himself leaves his mark on the architecture of Paris. François Mitterand left the glass pyramid at the Louvre, and Spreckelsen's triumphal arch in the new neighbourhood of La Defense. The current president Nicolas Sarkozy has taken up the legacy of Napoleon, who with the aid of Baron Haussmann cut Paris up into the districts we know today with large squares and wide boulevards. In June 2008 President Sarkozy invited ten of the world's leading architects to submit proposals for a re-establishment of Paris as a unified city – a re-design at the master-plan level with the aim of unifying Paris, which is today arranged like a fried egg: the yolk is the core Paris we know as tourists, the white is the suburbs – the *arrondissements*, where the majority of the citizens of Paris live. The suburbs are cut off from the centre by the ring road *la peripherique*, and some of them are best known for their desolate concrete landscapes and ghettoization.

10 Principles for Metropolitan Paris

Rogers Stirk Harbour + Partners,
Madrid/Barcelona/Tokyo/London

Rogers' plan for Paris builds a bridge between centre and periphery

With its proposal for a master plan to unify Paris, the Richard Rogers architectural office intends to build a bridge across the city's great psychological distances. Paris is split by the ring road that separates centre from suburbs typified by concrete and ghettos. According to Rogers the great inequality and psychological distance between the various parts of the city are the greatest challenge for Paris. His team proposes to begin by covering the railway tracks that divide up the city and creating a network of fertile parks instead. In this way a continuous green belt will connect centre and periphery, and beneath it technology will be concealed that can ensure alternative energy for the Paris of the future with less CO_2-emission. At the same time Rogers proposes an expansion of public transport and a transformation of socially disadvantaged areas such as Clichy-sous-Bois, where violent rioting broke out in 2005. A mixed population composition is crucial to the development and cohesion of the city.

Pari(s) Plus petit

MVRDV, Rotterdam

MVRDV's vision for Greater Paris 2030
The project *Pari(s) Plus petit* by MVRDV stands for "more" on less space: Greater Paris needs both more responsibility and an ambition to continue its development and build a solid base for an even more remarkable city. MVRDV's plan in collaboration with ACS and AAF for the Greater Paris area consists of several elements.

'The Synthesis', defining the spatial agenda for the city, proposes a series of 17 large-scale interventions. The goal is to make Paris highly accessible, for instance by creating a new central station at Les Halles, and by adding a new metro line and two underground motorway ring roads. This, together with the creation of new 'Grand Axes' and a buried infrastructure along the Seine, liberates space for new urban living in a green environment. Further elements of the vision are investments in transport, nature, education, culture, social cohesion and vast amounts of renewable energy. As a whole the projects can prevent future sprawl and radically transform Paris into one of the densest, most compact and therefore most sustainable, high-quality cities in the world: *Pari(s) Plus petit*.

MVRDV has developed various web-based tools for planning sustainable cities: "The City Calculator©" can quantify the "performance and behaviour" of the new city; "The Data" provides an overview of the detailed research; and "The Observations" is a series of articles on the history, the issues and the potentials of the French metropolis.

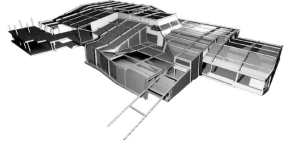

Cities as living organisms

As many cities continue to grow at great speed and become denser and denser, problems arise with pollution and a shortage of recreative areas. The green features of the city provide shade, purify and cool the air, create biodiversity, ensure access to water and thus help to improve mankind's mental and physical wellbeing.

Cities can be seen as organisms that live, breathe, grow and change like a plant or tree, so the city and the people in it should be viewed as part of nature, not as something contrary to nature. The challenge for dense cities with complex infrastructural networks and thousands of people filling the streets every day is to rethink the relationship between nature and the city, giving nature a new place, not necessarily as parks on the ground, but integrated in the buildings.

Sportplaza Mercator

Amsterdam, 2005-2006
Ton Venhoeven, Copijn, Utrecht

Roof and wall gardens make an important alternative contribution to a green urban environment. The Sportplaza Mercator in Amsterdam is an example of how a building can be given a green 'overcoat'. Copijn develops simple systems that can be used on almost all types of wall surface, indoors and outdoors, with variations on 50 different plants that change the look of the facade with the seasons. The Sportplaza Mercator in Amsterdam has been renovated in a collaboration between the architect Ton Venhoeven and Copijn and harmonized with the surrounding Rembrandt Park, which has been renovated with the focus on integrating new elements among the large trees.

The Vertical Garden – from nature to cities

Patrick Blanc, Paris

The Vertical Garden is composed of three parts: a metal frame, a PVC layer and a layer of felt. The metal frame is hung on a wall or may be self-supporting. A 1 cm thick PVC sheet is riveted to the metal frame. This layer gives the whole structure rigidity and makes it water¬proof. Watering and fertilization are automated, and come from the top. The weight of a vertical garden, including plants and metal frame, is less than 30 kg per square metre.

In any city, anywhere in the world, a naked wall can be turned into a vertical garden and thus become a valuable shelter for biodiversity. Vertical gardens, thanks to their thermal insulation effect, help to reduce energy consumption, both in winter by protecting the building from the cold, and in summer by providing a natural cooling system.

The Vertical Garden is also an efficient way of purifying the air. The felt in them attracts pollutant particles in the air and slowly decomposes and mineralizes them before they end up as plant fertilizer.

Besides photosynthesis, light and carbon dioxide, plants only need water and the many minerals dissolved in it. Soil is not really necessary: wherever water is available all year long, for example in tropical or temperate mountain forests, plants can grow on rocks, tree trunks and soil-less slopes. In Malaysia, for instance, some 2,500 of the 8,000 known plant species grow without any soil.

Ecomimesis

Ken Yeang, London/Ampang

The architect Ken Yeang has formulated an architectural philosophy he calls 'ecomimesis', which means that architecture imitates nature's ecosystems to create a balance between organic and inorganic mass. Yeang sees this approach as architecture's contribution to a global solution to the world's resource scarcity and climate problems. Architecture designed according to ecological principles should also reflect this visually. According to Yeang, a 'green' building should look green and express the climate and vegetation of the place. This is a natural consequence of his working process, in which he analyses the qualities of the place in terms of ecological and natural conditions and evaluates the energy requirements of the building, its potential for producing its own energy, its light, sound and air quality etc. with the goal of balancing comfort, aesthetics and functionality in a design integrated with the local vegetation.

IT Park Millenium Spire,
Manesar, Gurgaon, Indien
T.R. Hamzah & Yeang Sdn. Bhd.

Solaris, Fusionopolis, Phase 2B, Singapore
T.R. Hamzah & Yeang Sdn. Bhd.

EDITT Tower, Singapore
T.R. Hamzah & Yeang Sdn. Bhd.

Rooftop Farming

Liuzhou, Guangxi Zhuang, 2005
Cradle To Cradle
William McDonough & Michael Braungart,
Charlottesville

This master concept suggests, through design strategies, a future that is positive and hopeful in all respects. In an endeavour to maximize social engagement, the plan creates an urban structure that promotes walking and healthy activity in its multitude of parks, paths and trails. The development will also preserve existing stream and wetland communities, returning clean, healthy water to the ecosystem at the same rate and in the same patterns as the undeveloped site through the use of integrated strategies. In keeping with its status as a demonstration project, the plan shows what is possible in Liuzhou in China as well as communities around the globe.

Design Strategies
- Construction of green roofs to provide storm water management and reduce energy costs.
- Biogas collected from human waste used for cooking and saleable electricity.
- Easily accessible public transport (Rapid Transit Bus) using low-emission technology.

I'M LOST IN PARIS

Paris, 2008

Architect: R&Sie(n) Paris
Creative team: François Roche, Stéphanie Lavaux, Jean Navarro
Hydroponic system: R&Sie(n)
Dimensions: 130 m²
Location: Confidential
Client: Confidential
Cost: Confidential
Structural development and construction of the green prototype: Christian Hubert De Lisle & Cie
Glass beakers: Pedro Veloso (consultant: Vanessa Mitrani)
Ferns: Dryopteris felix-Mas

Scenario
1. Design of a private laboratory as a 'duck-blind cabana'
2. 1200 hydroponic ferns
3. 300 blown glass-beaker components for bacterial culture (Rhizobium genus) to increase the nitrogenization percentage without chemical manure / extra light through refraction / 'Rear Window' relationship with the neighbourhood opposite with views of enclosed courtyard
4. Collection of rain for watering plants with individual mechanical drop-by-drop system including dosage control for nutritional supplements
5. 'Devil's Rock' outcrops (for *Close Encounters of the Third Kind*) with nature (ferns) from the Devonian (dinosaur) period, technologically domesticated to come back in the current regressive French period.

This is the story of an urban witch living behind a rear window designed like a duck-blind cabana. Like an alchemist, she feeds the plants with a drop-by-drop hydroponic system with watering fluid coming from a bacterial chemical preparation in 200 beakers and disseminated over the fern surfaces.

R&Sie(n)'s own home base in Paris was designed with great attention to the character and physical conditions of the place. With words and pictures from films, literature and philosophy, *imlostinparis* is a textbook example of R&Sie(n)'s architectural method; the specific features of the place are viewed as a potential and afterwards function as a design principle.

With its placing on the ground floor in a yard surrounded by higher apartment blocks in the middle of Paris, it has been important to protect the dwelling from the curious gaze. 'Rear Window' refers to Hitchcock's film of the same name, where the protagonist lives by viewing the life of his neighbours.

The green-plant screening, like all other green spaces in the city, functions as an air purifier, oasis and recreative space, but because of the association with the film *Close Encounters of the Third Kind* the vegetation is at the same time viewed as an alien element in the middle of the man-made city; a UFO from another planet – or just a fern, a species that has survived for more than 300 million years – that both attracts and repels passers-by: *imlostinparis* is an architectural attraction and at the same time a place the residents of the dwelling can keep to themselves.

Vertical greenhouse – preserve through growth!

Copenhagen, 2009
Tanja Jordan Arkitekter og Kirsten Birk M.A.A., Copenhagen.

An alternative energy renewal of existing brick multi-storey housing, Nordhavnsgården, 1935.
A high percentage of the existing building mass in Denmark is facing imminent renewal and calls for an optimization of the energy performance. Many housing projects are multi-storey brick constructions, out of date in terms of indoor climate and plan arrangements, and face a clear challenge: for example how to preserve the architectural qualities of the buildings despite traditional renovation projects, which often destroy the tactile and architectural expression of the brick construction by cladding it with a thick layer of insulating material.

The project shows how the existing building mass can be viewed as a material that can be modified and worked with. The exhibition model therefore also functions as a transformable entity without a definitive idiom, as a facade where the public is actively involved in its design.

The project develops a sustainable alternative by adding to and expanding the solid Danish building tradition in the form of diversified apartment sizes, improved light access and indoor climate, new types of collectivities and green outdoor spaces.

The establishment of a glass screen on the south side of the building creates a climatic buffer zone where passive solar heat has a positive effect on the building's heating costs. Vertical shafts create natural ventilation and an inflow of pre-heated air to the apartments. Plants in this intermediate space add a vertical green growth room for the occupants of the building.

The energy consumption of the building is less than Low-Energy Class 2, which is standard for new construction.

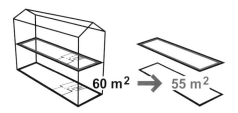

60 m² → 55 m²

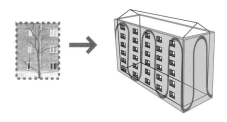

conventional energy refurbishment destroys the original qualities of the brick constructions

+ m²

+ ∿∿∿

+ 🌱

+ **community**

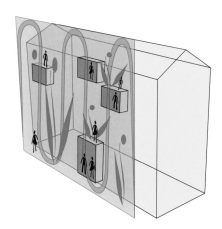

new energy refurbishment must develop alternative ways to optimize the energy consumption of existing brick constructions

Maison Latapie

Floirac, 1993
Anne Lacaton & Jean Philippe Vassal, architects, Sylvain Menaud, architect and with Cesma, IngÈrop, engineers, Paris

This inexpensive house is the result of a commission to build, on a low budget, a house for a couple with two children.

Located in a discontinuous residential area, the house fits into the street profile. It consist of a simple volume on a rectangular base that supports two open platforms. On a metal frame, one half, on the street side, is covered with opaque fibre-cement sheeting; the other half, on the garden side, is covered with transparent polycarbonate sheeting, forming a conservatory. A wooden volume clamped into the frame behind the opaque sheeting defines a heated, insulated winter space opening on to the conservatory and the street-side exterior. The conservatory faces east and gets the early morning sun. It is an inhabitable part of the house, equipped with ample ventilation panels for comfort in summer. The mobile nature of the east and west facades enables the house to change from its most closed to its most open state according to the need and desire for light, transparency, intimacy, protection and ventilation. The inhabitable part of the house can vary with the seasons, from the smallest unit with living room and bedrooms to the largest by integrating the entire garden in high summer. The house thus functions as a third climate-screen for human beings – the skin is the first, then comes our clothing, and then the walls of our dwelling. The Latapie house requires human interaction, which makes it less static and requires fewer if any fixtures for heating and cooling. Just as we regulate our clothing to adapt to temperature changes, the house should be regarded as an extra garment that serves human comfort. The climate screen as well as the human interaction are important elements of the profile of the Latapie house.

Plus

Frederic Druot, Anne Lacaton
& Jean-Philippe Vassal, Paris

In France major public urban renewal programmes are being initiated, involving the demolition of the existing public housing estates from the 1960s and 1970s. At the same time there is still a great need for public housing. Druot, Lacaton & Vassal have formulated an architectural concept with the focus on unexploited quality potential that will result in more economical and efficient housing.

The PLUS concept focuses on improving existing housing projects in all areas, with the inherent qualities of the place as the point of departure. Instead of demolition and rebuilding, the architects urge constant rethinking about the 'plus sides': additions, changes and recycling – transformation of the existing potential. The aim is to set a new standard for large city apartments bathed in daylight, variation in the dwelling typologies, user and service functions and communal areas.

Druot, Lacaton & Vassal propose an alternative strategy based on the PLUS philosophy, choosing to improve and expand the existing apartments to meet individual needs. The transformation consists of extending the living space and adding extra surfaces such as balconies. Walls out to balconies can be opened and windows can be installed to provide daylight and views.

The Bois-le-Prêtre building is part of a high-rise project built in the sixties along the ring motorway of Paris. The goal is, within the existing structure, to free up the individual apartments and provide more daylight, air and a larger living area. The apartments are enlarged by adding new 'decks' around the building, making the rooms larger and permitting winter gardens and balconies. The residents will gain new communal areas as well as the option of choosing new apartment types.

The new decks will be built with prefabricated elements mounted on site on a steel structure. In the expanded area a winter garden and balcony will be installed. Traditional windows will be changed to glass sliding walls. The unheated winter gardens will be furnished with transparent polycarbonate facade elements functioning as double facades that can be opened and will have a warm and acoustically insulating effect.

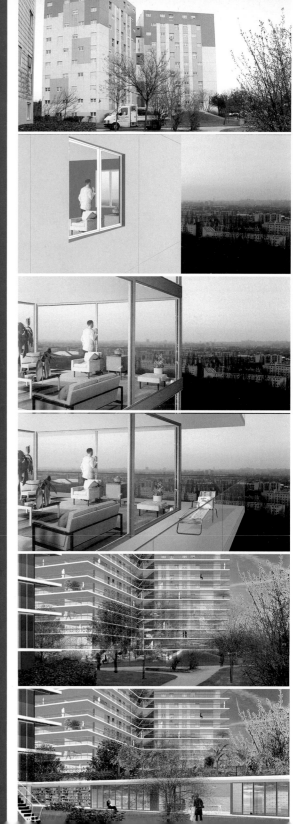

Favela la Rocinha

Rio de Janerio
Frederic Druot Architecture, Paris

Favela Rocinha has been transformed in accordance with Druot's PLUS concept, which focuses, with its starting-point in the inherent qualities of the place, on additions, changes and recycling – a transformation of existing possibilities rather than demolition, rebuilding and thus unnecessary resource consumption.

The *favelas* are densely built-up slum areas in the cities of Brazil, often on the outskirts of the city and up mountainsides. The houses of a favela have been built by the occupants themselves from available material, and grow with the terrain as required. In its basic concept the favela is therefore sustainable, while the health and energy conditions are often poor. These conditions can be improved significantly through better utilization of the potential of the terrain, the reorganization of the service functions and an independent energy supply.

Favela Rocinha is on hilly terrain where horizontal construction optimizes the exploitation of natural light sources and minimizes the formation of shadows inside. Druot's philosophy adheres to the dense-low type of construction known from both Moroccan desert villages and Danish suburbs. On the basis of a detailed analysis of the existing structure of the area and its settlements, Druot has developed a phased plan where usable structures are preserved, vulnerable areas are adapted and unsafe constructions are converted and re-used. This means that the residents of the favela can be offered larger dwelling areas, optimum light penetration, landscape and comfort, more service functions and a better view.

Work is being done on several coordinated measures that will enable the development of a waste-based energy supply (biogas and electricity), recycling of construction materials and equipment for do-it-yourself projects as well as the establishment of a communal rainwater system.

Carlsberg – our city – our urban spaces

Copenhagen, 2007
Entasis, Copenhagen

The site is an old industrial ground with a large amount of historical buildings. Carlsberg Breweries were based here from 1847 until late 2008 when the production moved, leaving a 33 ha site close to the Copenhagen centre.

The main thesis of the project is based on the urban spaces and the existing historical build-ings, of which some carry a very strong identity for the area and for the Carlsberg brand. *Carlsberg - our city*, therefore, means public- and shared space first, buildings second.

With a reconciliation of the density of the classic city and credible urban spaces - with state-of-the-art knowledge in sociology, architecture, art and engineering – the vision for a future city is created. Carlsberg wants to be in the lead and show the way for a socially, economically and environmen-tally sustainable city. Sustainability on Carlsberg is based on a series of relations, which each con-tribute to holistic picture of the good city; a city which optimizes the framework for a good and responsible life for the individual. The city is a complex size, presenting actions which range i.e. from minimizing consumption of energy in land-scaping and building to the design of safe and iden-tity-creating urban environments, from local han-dling of water to offering nearby green, recreative outdoor spaces, from reusing building materials and existing buildings to varying housing types.

The complexity is therefore the basis, but also the goal. The sustainability on Carlsberg is the sum of the many actions, individually crucial, but only making sense when they are concluded in an overall completed work.

The base of the idea is the 'sustainability in all its aspects'-mindset and with the approach that the city is for the people. At the same time planning is done with respect towards the spirit of the place and the existing historical elements of the place, and great attention is put into creating a close relationship with the surrounding city.

Nordholmene Urban Delta

Copenhagen, 2009
COBE, SLETH Modernisn, Rambøll, Copenhagen

The Nordhavnen industrial landscape consists today of angular quay facilities and wide open expanses in the large space of the Øresund, and marks the sailing channel into Copenhagen Harbour. The area has a long history which must not be obliterated in the conversion process, and offers great recreative potential. Access to the natural landscape has therefore been given high priority in the planning of Nordhavnen, where 40,000 residents can live close to nature.

Environmental sustainability is a central concern of the planning. The choice of centralized rather than decentralized energy solutions is rooted in Danish tradition. Wind power, geothermal heating, seawater cooling, marine biomass and energy-efficient buildings all help to create the basis for a CO_2-negative neighbourhood.

At Nordholmene it is easier to walk, cycle or use public transport than to use the car. A green corridor for an overhead metro or other collective traffic will link the islets with one another. The stations are to be placed so that most residents will have less than 400 metres to the nearest stop. Along 'The Green Loop' a direct bicycle path will be laid out, making it easy to cycle. It will thus be possible to reach local shopping outlets, workplaces, cultural facilities – or public transport that will take residents there – within a five-minute walk from each home.

The strategy for Nordholmene is not about transferring the lifestyle of the suburbs to an area that belongs to the city – on the contrary, it is about giving the Copenhageners the option of settling in a healthy neighbourhood in the heart of the city.

The quays have been made accessible so residents can get down to the water, across the water, sail on the water or swim in the water. The possibilities are harbour bathing, tidewater steps, rowing clubs, floating markets, corbelled plateaux, pontoon bridges, slipways, homes on the water, shortcuts across basins and the like.

Curitiba

1971-1983
Jaime Lerner Institute, Curitiba

Curitiba in southeastern Brazil faced explosive urban growth from the 1950s onward. Its metropolitan population mushroomed from a town of 300,000 in 1950 to a metropolis of 1.5 million in 1990, making it Brazil's fastest growing city.

The approach of the architect and mayor of Curitiba, Jaime Lerner, to the revitalization of cities depends on what he calls "urban acupuncture", which involves pinpointed interventions that can be accomplished quickly to release energy and create a positive ripple effect. Since his first term in office (1971-1975), there has been a conscious decision to take control of the city's urban growth process by using two basic tools: land use legislation in combination with the right to determine public transport routes. Total priority was given to public transport throughout the entire city and to pedestrians in the Central Area.

The plan involved a new road design that would minimize traffic: the Trinary Road System. This uses two one-way streets moving in opposite directions, surrounding a smaller, two-lane street where the express buses have their exclusive lane. Five of these roads form a star that converges on the city centre. This led to the world's first bus-based Mass Transport Network, including the 'tube' stations and the 25-metre bus units that operate as a Metro.

Instead of technologically sophisticated solutions Curitiba chose to refuse to build an underground metro system, which would otherwise have cost 90 million dollars per kilometre. The express busway system came in at 200,000 dollars per kilometre, and the savings were invested in other priority areas, such as the city's huge garbage problem.

Under the "garbage that isn't garbage" programme, 70% of the city's trash is recycled by its residents. Once a week, a truck collects paper, cardboard, metal, plastic and glass that has been sorted in the city's homes.

Everything in Curitiba started with the children, the theory being that if they understood their city, they would respect it better. In every school, children were taught how to sort the garbage, and

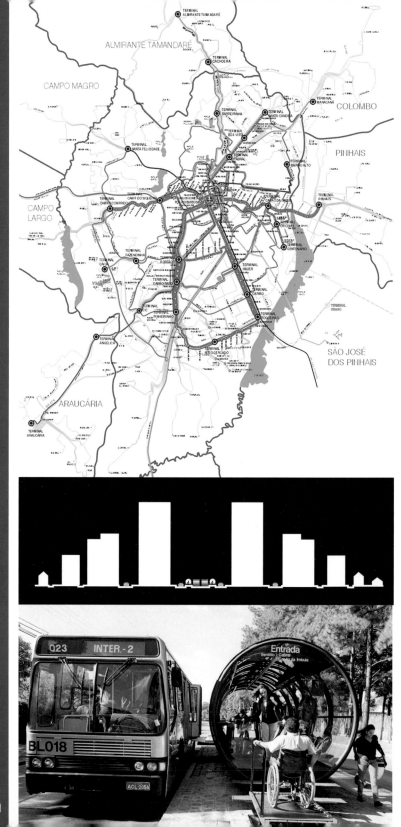

the children taught their parents. So that is why, for almost 20 years since 1989, the city of Curitiba has had the highest rate of garbage sorting in the world – 70%.

Designing with nature

Flooding was one of the most serious problems that Curitiba faced. The city centre used to have frequent floods, the effects of which were worsened by the construction of houses and other structures along stream and river basins. Necessary drainage works had to be dug underground at a very high cost. From the early 1970s, some strips of land were set aside for drainage, and certain low-lying areas were put off-limits for building purposes. The stream protection strips were developed as linear parks and supported by comprehensive tree planting. The proportion of green areas leapt from half a square metre to 52 square metres per inhabitant.

Biesbosch Stad

Rotterdam, 2005
Michel Desvigne & Christine Dalnoky, Paris

The natural infrastructures of cities
What does the 'reading' of a large area have to do
with the transformation of contemporary cities?
Our landscapes today are often the product of
technocratic regulations. Consolidation of farmland and extensive farming have led to the disap-
pearance of physical elements (embankments,
hedges, and drains) that gave the landscape its
legibility.

In the case of Biesbosch Stad, Rotterdam, the
areas to be transformed extend over dozens of
kilometres. The goal is to attain the dimensions of
nature once more: yet the play on the imprint of
water arises from complete artifice. The former
rivers become embankments, the embankments
are transformed into residential areas: the whole
ensemble derives from forms in nature that are
not copied or brought back, but transposed.

Map 1
The idea is to break the dikes to allow the water
(shown in dark grey) to spill out unimpeded in
the event of flooding. The materials from the
dismantled dikes would then be placed on the
imprint of the former rivers. Their sandy, non-
compactable beds would thus be raised, accent-
ing the observed inversion and forming areas that
are out of the water (indicated in light grey and
white). The widest surfaces are spaces on which
one can build (in white). The resulting landscape,
while susceptible to flooding, would continue to
be farmland.

Map 2
One is reminded of the Stockholm archipelago,
where magnificent scenarios are set in motion,
from one façade to the next, separated not by
avenues but by the presence of water. In the
same way, the Rotterdam project is built on
dense neighbourhood units, indicated on the plan
in brown; on circulation paths (in white); but also
on parks that look out over one another above
the floodable farmland.

Three basins on this site supply drinking water
to Rotterdam. Today they are cut off by polders. It
is essential to create new pathways for the water
flow, in case the water level rises around these
'lakes', whose branching rivers can be linked to
the new city via built embankments.

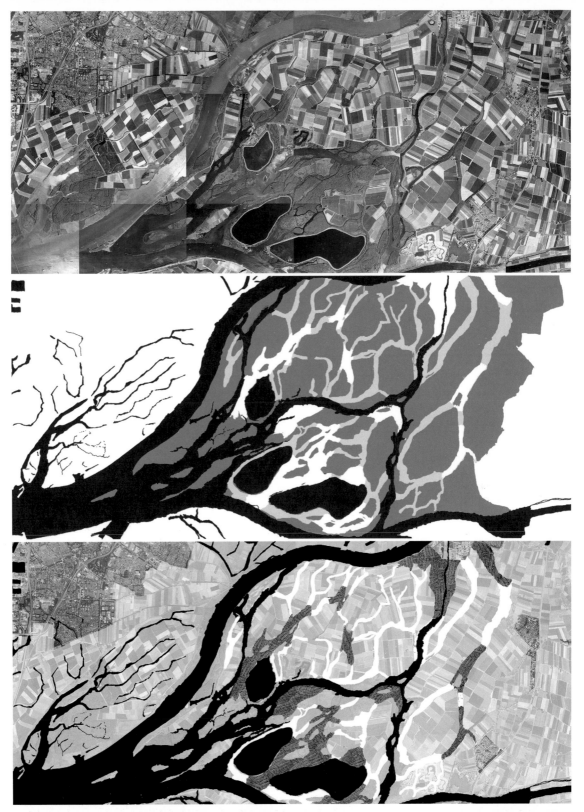

LAB II

Masdar City

The sustainable city of the future
Foster + Partners

Foster + Partners are showing their ongoing planning of a brand new city in the United Arab Emirates.
Masdar City is a CO_2-neutral, waste-free city based
on lessons learned from the sustainable structure
of the medieval city as well as the latest climate
technology. The city will house just under 50,000
residents, and the buildings are no taller than five
storeys. The density is high and with just 200 metres
between each transport link, the city is completely
car-free. With inspiration from Arab culture and
building customs, it integrates wind towers and
solar cells that supply energy and ventilation for the
natural cooling of the desert city. The first construction phase has started: the 60 MW solar-cell power
plant that is to supply energy for the building of the
rest of the city. The laboratory monitors Foster +
Partners' studies and work with the sustainable city
of the future.

Foster and Partners
Interview with Stefan Behling and Gerard Evenden

By Peter Andreas Sattrup

PAS: I'd like to talk about your work with sustainability, especially your work with energy-optimized architecture. How do you view the relationship between architecture and energy?

SB: One of the most important things to understand is that consumption is a question of demand, and demand is dependent on design. Your demand for petrol depends on the design of your car, and your demand for a car depends on how the city you live in is designed. So if you can change that, you can change your consumption in the end. The same goes for buildings: it applies to all sorts of things. Architecture and planning can reduce the demand for energy through the way buildings, infrastructure and urban development work. One of the important points is that architects deal with buildings, and 44% of the world's energy consumption is related to buildings; 34% goes on transport. The way a city is designed affects your need for energy for transport. A resident of Copenhagen only consumes a ninth of the energy a resident of Detroit consumes, even though the two cities are in more or less the same climate zone.

There's a graph that shows how petrol consumption is directly dependent on the density of cities.
SB: Exactly: Newman and Kenworthy's studies of the relationship between energy consumption on transport and the density of the world's major cities. There's a relationship between sustainability and economy at all levels. Thinking about the way you organize your building, its shape and orientation, gives you the maximum environmental benefit, but costs very little. The form of the building mass is crucial to its energy consumption. If you go up a level, and for example start making sun screens, you can also save a lot of energy, but then it starts to cost a lot of money. And in the end you can put solar cells on it and install the latest in intelligent engineering technology, but that costs even more money.

Look at things from the opposite angle: start with a 'dumb' building and you can put as many solar cells on it as you like – it won't work. The same applies if you choose to put your building in the wrong place. It's like aircraft or cars: if they have the wrong shape, they just won't do.

What's the biggest challenge?
You've got a migration of people from the countryside to the cities throughout most of the world, and that development will continue for many years to come, even though local developments in China, for example, may go the other way. In the longer term the cities will get bigger. In twenty years the urban population percentage of China has risen just as much as it did in 200 years in Europe. But in Europe the great challenge will mainly be what to do with the existing buildings. You can't play the game of changing the form, which might take you more critical of actually keeping the building. You can throw as much technology and just as much money as you like at a wretchedly designed sixties building, it'll still be a useless building.

But surely you also have to make allowances for the energy that has already been invested in the buildings?
GE: Yes, but the embedded energy (energy used for material production and the construction of buildings) only accounts for a modest share of the energy used in the building in the course of its life. If you design a building badly and it has to be torn down after 20 years because it's unsuitable, can't be upgraded and therefore can't be used any more, then it makes no difference at all whether your energy consumption on materials has been low. You will have to design the building so it's flexible and can have a long life, and that includes assessing the relationship between materials and energy. You can for example choose materials that have taken a lot of energy to produce, but which extend the life cycle

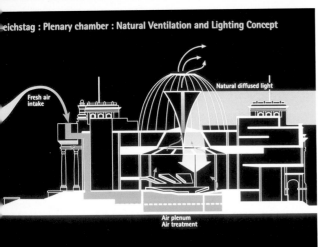

eichstag : Plenary chamber : Natural Ventilation and Lighting Concept

Natural diffused light

Fresh air intake

Air plenum
Air treatment

considerably. It could even happen that after 50 or 100 years these materials will have increased in value because they are recyclable, so it can be a good investment to choose expensive materials in the longer term. The important thing is the totality, the overall design.

In European cities it's a huge challenge to find this balance – including when you consider that many buildings represent cultural heritage?
GE: A London town house is an example of a building type that has been able to change over the past 200 years. A Georgian town house may be a dwelling for a single-family, while the identical building next door perhaps contains sixteen different flats. A sustainable city is an integrated city.

SB: There's also the argument for mixing functions: a perfect building could be a workplace today, a home tomorrow, an artists' collective the next day, because they can't afford anything else. So the artists help to create a better city neighbourhood, then later rich bankers move in once the neighbourhood has become smart enough. If a building can live throughout centuries in that way, it is by definition a good building. Older buildings are as a rule very flexible. Many newer buildings on the other hand are difficult to change, and some of them are even really hard to make energyefficient. Which of these buildings are worth preserving? That's a big question that brings us back to the question of energy and how much waste you create by tearing them down.

So your argument is that the form and orientation of the building, its openness to future changes, is simply the most important thing in the decision-making hierarchy – because it's a matter of reducing the energy demand and consumption?
GE: Yes, if you don't reduce the demand, none of the technologies of today can create enough energy to run the building. You have to reduce the energy demand by working with orientation and with the passive systems of the buildings.

That points back to a design reality that is all about form. It sound like a fine situation for architects – after all, that's what architects would prefer to work with?
GE: The interesting thing about SwissRe, Commerzbank and the Reichstag in Berlin is not that they are

iconic buildings because of their form or architectural character. The interesting thing is that everything in them has a function, and that function is driven by studies of the sun, the light, the movements of the air, the place, the way people occupy the building, their needs ... That's what drives the form of the buildings, and that's what gives them their iconic nature.

You mention the forces of nature as a primary formative element in architecture.
SB: Of course, that's how it's been since the dawn of time.

But it would appear that this point has been rather pushed into the background when you look at the architecture of the last few generations?
SB: There are some quotes that can illustrate those developments. Buckminster Fuller said: "Do more with less". And you have "Form follows function", which I think Mies meant in a quite special way. Today I would call it "Form follows performance". The performance of the building is crucial. How good is your building when it comes down to it? Buckminster Fuller also asked "How much does the building weigh?" Today the question is "How does it perform?" You expect a plane to fly well. It's the goal for a plane that it can stay in the air and be energy-efficient; that it doesn't hit the ground too fast if the engine cuts out. You also have a clear idea of how a good yacht has to perform. What should a building's performance criteria be? Those things have to be defined in terms of energy and sustainability. But buildings are only the top of the iceberg. Infrastructure and transport are the nine tenths below the surface. If you believe we should change the world, that people should live sustainably, you have to relate to the city and the infrastructure. You can't solve the problem with buildings alone.

– But how does that fit in with the buildings being a tenth of the problem, but using 44% of the energy?
SB: If you addtransportation, a total of 70% of energy consumption depends on buildings, the way people move among buildings, and the way the infrastructure works.

You have to look at the underlying system.
SB: Exactly. We talked about the relationship between the density of the city and energy consump-

tion: it's a complex relationship. Mankind has been developing cities for 10,000 years. It isn't an individual human being's idea or design, it's something humanity has developed as a good way to let many people live together. Behind the Roman city, behind the medieval city, there are a range of logics, and most of them are related to the human body, especially the legs. Long, short, thick, thin legs – there are walking distances that are optimal for human beings. Bed sizes, chair sizes, there are simply scales that work for the city.

Salvador Dalí once expressed his contempt for the metric system. For him measurements that were originally body-based – feet, inches, spans etc. – were the only meaningful ones?
SB: Yes, those are the measurements of which architecture was originally formed, and in the English-speaking part of the world some are still in use. But the way a city functions also points towards economics. If you want a city where you can walk along to the shops or to a bazaar, there are certain walking distances that are acceptable. They can vary by a few hundred metres, depending on the climate. If you want a city with mixed functions, it will have to be dense. There's a threshold value, a critical mass of a few thousand people who have to be able to move around in the area if you want to keep a shop. Otherwise there aren't enough people within walking distance. If you look at the American suburbs, the so-called 'urban sprawl' – the local shopping scene is dying there. In the end you only have the big shopping malls that make it necessary for people in a very large area to drive a car to shop. The point is that there is the traditional city, and the there's the modern, car-dependent city ...

GE: ... which has also destroyed the community of the city, since the walking distances are too long and the connections are thus broken ... in urban development you have to address the future development of transport. The car won't exist forever in its present form. A city like London has developed around traffic with horse-drawn carriages, in Rome it's even denser, more based on pedestrians. What happens is that the transport system adapts to the cities. In Rome you see many more small cars and scooters than you do in Detroit. If you can change the way transport takes place, decrease the area it takes up, you can also change the city environment.

Our problem is that we have let transport become the driving force behind the development of the city.

SB: People have been willing to give up the city limits and let the city spread, because it only meant a few minutes more in the car. What you should say is, the city ends, and there should be a very good reason if you're to be allowed to build farther out. Instead of building yet another business complex on a bare field, you should build on the basis of the railway lines, the bus station. Build where there are public transport options. It may be necessary to have incentives, since it's more expensive to build in places like that, and much cheaper to build in the countryside.

But it would be well connected and efficient. In terms of travelling time, you could also argue that it would benefit property development ...
SB: If you want everybody to have villas with a garden and a pool, you'll get motorways and traffic as a consequence. Monaco and Hong Kong have a very high density with 16-17,000 inhabitants per square kilometre, and some people might think that's too much. But this idea that high density is unattractive and associated with poverty is a bit of a myth. We live in a culture where the dream of the 'villa' is constantly promoted on TV. It's like commercials for burgers and cola. I'm not sure that people are born with an extreme desire for burgers. Notting Hill in London (a neighbourhood with large communal gardens) is incredibly dense with about 13,700 residents per square kilometre. The houses are around 200 years old, and it's one of London's most attractive neighbourhoods. New city areas in Britain are built with a density of 4,800 inhab./km^2. That's crazy when we have Notting Hill as a model that people really like, and where people from all over the world want to live.

Sustainability is also about values and culture?
GE: Many people have an image of sustainable architecture as something to do with plants and solar cells all over it. Lots of doodahs everywhere. But it's much more important to create a place for people that they can relate to. If that doesn't succeed, no one will accept it.

Your plan for Masdar City is an urban development project for a research city in Abu Dhabi in the United Arab Emirates. What was the angle of approach to that job?

GE: It was important for us to prove that it is possible to create cities without CO^2 emission and without waste. So we imposed the limitation on ourselves that all energy and all garbage was to be generated and treated within the area we had been assigned. It was important not just to prove it, but also to do it visibly, so people begin to think about what it is we do.

You could say that visibility becomes a cultural driving force that can get people to change their behaviour?
GE: Yes, and the statement must be strong enough to make people ask why we've done what we did. We've studied historic city patterns in the desert. They were all compact, originally for defensive reasons, but the compactness, the density and the relationship with the surrounding land gave them some interesting climatic qualities. The projections on the houses and the angles in the streets produce turbulence and help to cool the air. And you can use all that knowledge to create a new city. So we laid out two square shapes as a city structure within an area of 7 square kilometres, surrounded by an open area for the production of solar energy, waste water plant etc. so that the open area can maintain the whole energy supply and the waste treatment in the new city. People ask why we didn't just build up the whole area, and the answer is that this is the balance you have to think about in the future. The intention of the master plan is also to generate new ideas. It's a bit like Central Park in New York, except that in this case the park is around the city.

So the surrounding area for technical facilities has also been conceived as a recreative area?
GE: Certainly – there are recreative areas between the technical functions.

The plan recalls the medieval cities where crops were cultivated just outside the city wall. In this case it's energy that is cultivated and waste that is recirculated?
GE: All cities have a hinterland where the supplies come from. We would also have liked areas for the production of food, but we didn't have enough area to balance it with. Of course we had to match the measurements to our master plan in terms of what we had available. And there isn't enough area to produce food at the place. But the thinking is there. In the final analysis all cities and countries must think about the limits of urban development. Energy

for the city itself is also produced on the spot. The smaller square has a solar power plant that creates energy for the urban development of the large square, and which can later be taken down and become another stage of the city. The important thing the plan symbolizes is that there is a criterion, a limit to the growth of the city in relation to the surrounding area.

SB: There's a lot of talk about CO_2-neutral, sustainable cities. This will be the first city of that kind actually to be built.

GE: Masdar is to be a Silicon Valley for renewable energy. It's all about gathering researchers and getting the research started that we need. When the government of Abu Dhabi originally took the initiative for the Masdar project, they travelled around and they realized that the research in the field was scattered and unintegrated. There was plenty of good research, but no one was trying to gather it together, and there was a tendency to hold on to information for commercial reasons. To accelerate development it's necessary to create this place and bring people together. That's what the Masdar initiative is all about. The city is a means of facilitating this development.

SB: Abu Dhabi is using its present position to invest in the future. The vision comes from Abu Dhabi's leaders, and they are spending very great resources on realizing it. In just a few years they will have a great head start in know-how. Perhaps it isn't a bad comparison to think about NASA, which was kick-started when Kennedy decided we had to go to the Moon. There's an analogy with Venice, in terms of both density and spatial characteristics. But Venice also has the separation of traffic, where transport goes along the canals. If the streets run east-west you will have sun all day long. If they run north-south they will be in shade, and will look dreary. So by rotating the plan towards the south east/north west, we get this 'European' balance of changing daylight at special times of the day. That isn't 'energy thinking', it's about how we experience the city, its light, air and energy. It's a simple story, and it's important that the messages get out. The warm winds come from the sea direction, but the cool winds blow from the desert at night, since it cools down far faster. So we try to catch the cool winds

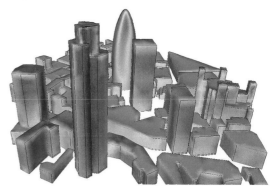

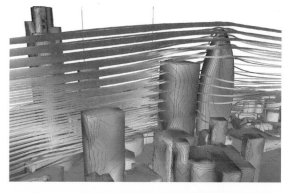

and create turbulence to maintain a pleasant micro-climate, by breaking up the directions.

So the geometry of the city becomes a passive cooling system that can lower the temperatures?
GE: Yes, and flush the streets through with fresh, cool air at night. In the morning the city will be heated up again. And that will affect the choice of materials for the buildings. You'll be able to use heavy materials with a high thermal mass where they lie in shade all day. If you put heavy materials in the sun they'll absorb so much heat that they will also radiate it inward. So the answer to that problem is insulation and foil-covered buildings where they're exposed to the sun. Everywhere we've drawn the ground floor back to create space and shade at ground level for the benefit of the pedestrians. The whole city is intended for pedestrians who move one deck above the motorized traffic. We have considered the development of transport systems in the future. Today you already have the technology for collision control in the cars, and the next step will be automated steering, driverless cars. But if you mix a system like that with the movements of human beings you can't control it, since humans are unpredictable and will reduce the efficiency of the system. That's why the deck is elevated 7 metres above the desert level, where the driving traffic is. All servicing of the city takes place below the deck, but the deck is reserved for pedestrians in traditional courtyard and street spaces.

That's like your initial argument about looking at the logic behind the whole transport system as a basis for design?
SB: Yes, but you must also understand that people won't give up the mobility they have as modern people. We want a system that can move us fast and conveniently. That has almost become a human right. No matter how much we like the traditional architecture, as in Bernard Rudofsky's *Architecture without Architects*, we can't just give up the cars and return to the past. We've got to give people something that's better than what they have now. That is fundamental to sustainability, otherwise people will just say no.

GE: So in Masdar City we've separated the systems so we have PRT (Personal Rapid Transport – driverless electric cars) below the deck, pedestrians and cyclists on the deck and a light rail track above the deck. Green areas are laid out so that 56% of the population have at most one minute's transport time to a square or one of the 'green lungs'. Cars can only come to the edge of the city, where you then have to change. Another advantage of raising the city up on a deck is that all installations come from below, so you will also be able to upgrade the city technologically without having to dig up the whole underground, which extends the lifetime of the city buildings and surfaces. We are also looking at how the city water is desalinated. There are no other possibilities. All the salt that is left over is a problem. At the moment it is just conducted out into the seawater, which increases the salt concentration and kills the local animal life in the sea. We are trying to develop building materials from salt, for example paving, so the problem will be turned into a positive factor.

SB: That's the next generation of research, to find out how cities can be supplied at all levels, and how much land area it takes up. For example it's incredibly complicated to find the balance between how far things we eat can be transported, and the energy it takes to produce them locally. Relative to London, tulips grown in greenhouses in Holland can be said to be 'locally produced', but in terms of energy could one consider importing tulips grown in a place that was warmer, but farther away? And in the end you could ask whether you need tulips at all out of season. Among researchers they talk about system boundaries. The system boundaries for a building are relatively simple, for a group of buildings or a city it gets far more complicated. As you change the scale the complexity increases by several dimensions.

If you look at the food that has to be produced to keep a city running, its ecological footprint, you need more than the 50% of the area that creates energy for Masdar City. You need to irrigate the desert or transport food to the city?
SB: But you also have to realize that everything has its limitations in terms of the reality we live in. Just now this is the place in the world where there is a will to push development. There will be others that want to accelerate it even more, but right now it's here.

GE: And compared with all the other projects people talk about, what is fundamentally different about Masdar is that it's real. We're building it. It has the funding. It's happening.

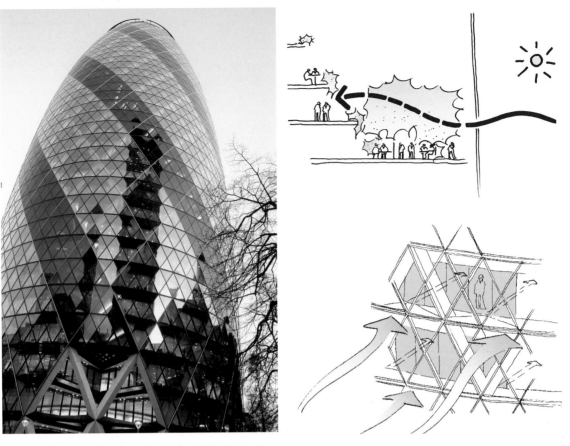

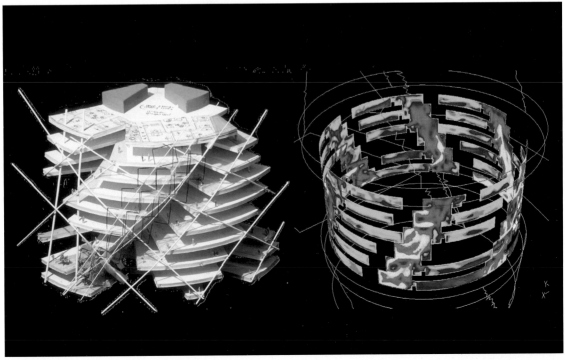

NATURE IS SILENT

By Ole Thyssen

There's big news and there's small news, and there's small news which, despite its unimpressive format, is still big. The kind that tells us that organic eggs are polluted with dioxin, or that the winter, for the third time running, is milder than the average.

And afterwards the world has changed. You've been buying free-range eggs, confident that they have no chemical dirt in them, so at least in one niche you could protect yourself against the evils of the world. That was an illusion. Nowhere in the world are you protected from the world.

Nature isn't the same either. Since the Enlightenment 'nature' has been a good thing – a refuge where you could slough off civilization and become one with your origins. Appeals to the 'natural' are as innumerable as the stars in the firmament, whether they're about whole-grain bread or shampoo, therapy or behaviour. Now civilization has forced its way into the heart of nature. The antithesis between nature and civilization has collapsed because civilization is no longer a ripple on the surface of nature. It is weighing nature down, not only locally, but globally. Our trust in nature as an inexhaustible resource and a recreative force has been shattered.

How can man protect himself against the manmade, which is turning against us like a hostile force? Everyone has to breathe, despite acid rain, exhaust fumes and dioxin; everyone has to eat, although nothing is sacred to industrial 'sophistication'; everyone has to live somewhere, even as the poles melt and the seas rise. In the global community, everyone depends on everyone else, and the state of the planet is our common destiny, even though the difference between rich and poor is also a difference in the capacity to protect yourself from disasters.

When danger looms, you have to do something. But what do you do when the danger is not local, but global? Where do you start? What can you – what can I – do to prevent global warming and melting?

When a task exceeds your strength you can run away from it. You can accept religion's offer of the Kingdom of God – free as it is from all earthly misery. That solution looks good in theory, but it poses problems in practice. Even with one foot in eternity you have to live on in time and, like Hamlet, in this harsh world draw thy breath.

When there is no liberation *from* the world, the liberation has to found *in* the world. And if you know something is wrong, you have to do something. If the problem is overconsumption, can you renounce your riches and, like Diogenes, live in a barrel, send your surplus to the poor and tickle your palate with turnips and black bread? It'll hard to get your family and friends to join you on that trip. Living in a barrel has no appeal for people who dream of living in a big way. And what use would it be if you were the only one? Your effort would be as conspicuous as a teardrop in the sea. "That gas you saved – I'm using it!", as the stickers on the SUVs say.

Clouds of fear
In the Middle Ages, said a Danish philosopher, Villy Sørensen, people believed in what they didn't know. Now we don't believe in what we know. We read every day that the planet is dying and needs to be saved fast. The perverse thing is that we've been hearing it for almost 50 years now, and the critical point is constantly being pushed forward towards a receding horizon. There's always time to make an effort, although it's urgent. But when it has been urgent long enough, you get used to the urgency and slacken the pace. You become immune to shrill media screams about imminent disaster.[1]

While the crisis of nature is a big theme in the media, it's a small theme in everyday life, where you don't take much notice of the ragged holes in the ozone layer or the massive CO_2 emissions. It's like terrorism. You know it's there, but there isn't a lot you can do about it, so your forget it.

Among the many fear themes that float like clouds above modern society and strike at random, one in particular stands out, because it's a source of many kinds of fear: the image of nature that has run amok in self-reinforcing chain reactions triggered by pollution and CO_2 emissions. The image of abused nature turning on us viciously is strong and penetrating because it's not only about 'nature out there' but also about 'nature in here' – our bodies, which are part of the great chain of nature and concern us in our innermost being.

Invisible proofs
The proofs are many, both visible and invisible. The visible ones include extreme weather conditions, belly-up fish, corals turning pale and forests withering. The invisible ones include the knowledge, or presumption, of dwindling resources, the ozone layer, rising temperatures and sperm cells with too short tails. And that little reservation 'presumption' is only there because, if you press people on the issue, they usually can't trace their knowledge back beyond the mass media that supply them with insight into the state of the world. As superficial connoisseurs of everything, we talk breezily about things we can neither see nor see through.

The nature of the mass media
The nature we can observe with our own eyes isn't the nature we meet in the mass media. They talk about nature as a whole, and no one has seen that. We meet it as figures and graphs, so we are informed and confused, disquieted and soothed. Agitated claims are met by back-pedalling counter-claims. Although it's easy to se through the soothing rituals of business people who want to appease consumers, or politicians who want to appease voters, the environmental organizations too have their agendas and have overdrawn the goodwill accounts they once had, with both overkill and wrong information. Even after Rachel Carson's prediction of a "silent spring" at the beginning of the 1960s, spring has come round every year in all its glory.

The information in the mass media is tailored so it can be understood by people with no special insight. It has to be taken on trust, because it can't be tested by direct observation or knowledge. And even when we know that the mass media spin and select, there isn't much we can do with our mistrust. We can't be everywhere and know everything. We live in two worlds that are difficult to connect, a life world and a media world.

Rhetorical proofs
When we, the public, don't know what we think we know, we become easy to manipulate. Experts and spokesmen don't only have to supply the public with information, they also have to know its ideas of happiness – what it wants to know, whether it is desire or fear that is stimulated. Side by side with the expert message, *logos*, we have the credibility, *ethos*, of the experts and advocates who talk about how bad things are. And the message is reinforced by the emotions, *pathos*, that are evoked when the message of imminent catastrophes is presented.

Experts and advocates too are subject to the urge to exaggerate to reach a public that has learned to protect itself against a surfeit of appeals. When the reports are too long and too difficult, the gap in insight must be filled with emotions. The public must be stirred up and put on Orange Alert. That is a short-sighted strategy that ends up making the public immune.

Loyalty and luxury

Being loyal means being prepared to act and to suffer. Except that it's hard to be loyal to something you don't know and can't see. The state of the planet is something remote and diffuse compared with the close demands of everyday life. If an effort for the state of the planet requires us to accept privations, the need for that effort must be conspicuous and the effect visible. Otherwise the will weakens. Symbolic measures like switching of the lights for an hour once a year, or turning off the water while you brush your teeth, seem faintly absurd.

Adam Smith's invisible hand worked because you simply had to obey your egoism and forget the totality. Unfortunately there are problems with the opposite version, where you have to obey the totality and forget your egoism. There's more power in the daily struggle to sustain and improve your life – the struggle for luxury. In modern societies, superfluity is a highly necessary thing, for the sake of both companies' sales and your own craving for recognition. This covers a multitude of loyalties with which the global environment cannot compete.

It may seem wrong to talk about loyalty as the opposite of luxury. But if loyalty is about action and passion, then it's true enough. We act and suffer so we can mollycoddle ourselves. But luxury is a relative concept. What is ordinary everyday life for the western suburbanite is unattainable luxury for the Indonesian au pair girl. The tune we dance to here is that no matter how rich we get, we'll never be rich enough: luxury is "the endless propagation of misery and need".[2] So, built into everyday life, there is a striving to improve it.

The image of luxury is also an image of living and building. The house isn't just a function that protects you from wind and weather. It's permeated by symbolism, because it's an outward image of who you are. So you invest your soul in your home. There is something contemptible about the small, said Kant, and Nietzsche wondered at the fact that "everything has grown smaller": "What can these houses be for? Truly, no great soul created them in his image".[3] That's why the house is an important showcase for displaying your strength and power. Public and private organizations build headquarters on which they lavish space, and private individuals squeeze their economy to the limit to live in the grand style. The house and its furnishings are a vital part of the dream of luxury.

Have: Fear and guilty conscience.
Wanted: Peace to live.

The alarming predictions of ecological collapse haven't materialized, so it's easy to claim that the state of nature isn't as black as it's painted. A public that has been frightened for years may have a hard time letting go of the familiar fear. But it's also tired of being fearful, and tired of demands that it should let its daily life be controlled by invisible things like the ozone layer and CO_2 emissions. It's tired of having a guilty conscience about living an ordinary life. That is the background for the apathy that meets the disturbing claims about threats that cannot be seen through and rendered visible, and which therefore cannot justify interventions in daily life.

The trust has gone. But normally you can do nothing with your mistrust but note that behind every description of nature lies a vested interest. When your knowledge is forced out on to thin ice, when radical adaptation is demanded, and when there's nothing specific you can do, there arises an uncertainty that fluctuates between fear and apathy.

Ban advertising?

If the problem is overconsumption of resources and energy, you can make a simple intervention. You can ban advertising, which stimulates consumption of things of which you have no elementary need, but which generate pleasure and recognition by others.

The stylized advertising images with beautiful people, houses, interiors and objects are a Paradisiac narcotic that confronts a godforsaken daily life and fills it with restlessness, cravings and shopaholism. So – no giant posters in the urban space, no skimpily clad models staring intensely at you from the newspaper pages, no avalanche of advertising brochures, no interruptions of TV films, no deafening ballyhoo.

You can already hear the rumbling on the horizon. Many voices united in furious protest with multifarious motives: aesthetic, moral, human considerations; rejection of the nanny state; freedom of speech; employment figures – everything is mobilized. Isn't this idea just despicable state coercion, interfering with the free market? Should public space be impoverished by mad iconoclasts, should the cities become sterile and puritan? Shouldn't we be allowed to live and let live as we wish? Shouldn't companies be allowed to express themselves as they want? And what about the sectors that will be driven to the wall? Won't it mean massive unemployment, not only in the advertising business but also in the media business, which lives on advertising revenue; in the garment industry, the perfume industry, the gadget industry, the automobile industry, the travel and tourism industries, the mineral water industry and .... anyone can open a newspaper, go for a walk in town or watch commercial TV to continue the list. Unemployment hits society selectively, so a ban on advertising would mean ruin, broken families and crying children. It would be nasty.

The dual imperative

For many years the western world has been plagued by two imperatives: an economic imperative that demands growth and employment, and an ecological imperative that demands lower, wiser consumption of raw materials and energy. The hope has been that the two can be reconciled, for example by sophisticated technology. But each time there is a conflict, the economics win. Politicians can't disappoint the voters' demands for wealth and welfare, and although the rumours of imminent ecological collapse fill the media, it is not experienced as a burning issue here and now. Unemployment and a failing economy are experienced much more palpably. The economic imperative can find support in a strong cycle that involves the public's desire for work, the business world's desire for sales, and the politicians' desire to be re-elected. Its juggernaut wheels have been created by everyone and no one, and seem impossible to stop.

The four paths

If we are to move on from here, we can follow four paths. The first takes an *epistemological* direction: does it make sense to talk about the destruction of nature? The second involves the *power of models*, and is about how we isolate and prioritize the innumerable causes that have led to the current state of the world. The third is the path of *responsibility*: how can we speak of blame and responsibility in relation to the state of nature? Does it make any sense at all

to get involved in the popular blame game? The fourth and last is the path of *action*: who can do something for the state of the planet, and why is it so hard to do what must be done?

Path 1: Epistemology

To say that nature is out of balance is a paradoxical statement. For when you have to argue for the claim, it emerges that the ruination or imbalance in nature is actually part of a good, natural order. There's nothing unnatural about ice melting, lowlands being flooded, fish dying, chromosomes mutating or rivers being filled with chemicals. Each individual change is not an invalidation, but a confirmation of the natural laws at which human beings have laboriously arrived. The dead lobsters in the slipstream of the factory effluents die in accordance with all the laws of nature, and the water they die in is not out of balance. On the contrary, it contains a very fine and complex balance of chemical compounds that just happen to be lethal for lobsters.[4]

Nature as norm

To say that a river is always in balance is not to deny that water can be toxic; it is just pointing out the pitfalls that are concealed by words like 'balance' or 'destroy'. They are not scientific words, they are words that are based on human ideas of what is good and bad. With words like 'imbalance' we refer indirectly to a privileged state that we call 'balance'. They may point back into the past – nature before the intervention of human beings, the Galapagos islands in 1835, when Darwin arrived there, agrarian society before industrialization. Or they may point forward to an accommodating future when nature is optimal for human wealth, understood here in the banal sense of consumption.

Nature in time

The image of ruined or destroyed nature accords beautifully with the succession of nature images we can trace throughout history: antiquity's eternal return of the same nature; Christianity's fallen and resurrected nature; the Renaissance's nature as the struggle of all against all; the Enlightenment's nature as an ideal balance; and Romanticism's nature as the invisible and mysterious foundation by which we are all borne up. All these images of nature have contributed fragments to the modern image of an endangered nature.

But these are images of nature, they are not nature itself, which is not only beyond good and evil, but also beyond concepts like 'rights', 'balance' and 'destruction'. Nature has as many rights over mankind as the mouse has over the cat. 'Right' is a concept mankind uses to observe with, not a concept that nature impresses on us. And the 'destruction' of nature is only a change from one state to another. It is also 'destruction' when flies are swatted, mice walk into traps or roses are sprayed against greenfly.

Path 2: The power of models

In local situations you can establish causes and effects with some degree of certainty, and in normal situations you can isolate unusual causes that trigger unusual effects. The test for whether a presumed cause is in fact a cause is that the effect vanishes if the presumed cause vanishes, and whether the cause has a 'suddenness' that makes it easy to identify. So you can often trace pollution 'upstream' to the factory, or food poisoning back to the bacteria and on to the chicken and the slaughterhouse. In theory it is also easy to trace the oil slick back to the ship that flushes out its tanks, although in practice it can be difficult to spot the ship and follow up on the matter.

Nature is silent, observers squabble

Delayed-action causes, or complex entanglements of causes, on the other hand, are hard to handle. In these cases it is not possible to furnish objective explanations and realistic descriptions, because that would exceed our limited capacity to gather and process data. Instead the breach is filled by assumption-based models that simplify and weigh probabilities.

This kind of model lies behind the claims about the state of the ozone layer, CO_2 emissions, fish stocks and nitrate leaching. The problem with this is that each choice of causes is subject to contingency: other causes could be selected, other weightings of the effects could be preferred. Although it is not possible to say just anything, it is possible to claim that causes and effects have been selected by an observer. Other observers may select and weigh them differently. Bluntly put, it is the observer who 'causes the causes' and thus also gives you the instructions on what can be done. Nature is silent. Observers squabble over how the tangled web of past causes and future effects is to be unravelled.[5]

Since we can't observe nature as a totality, we have to simplify, so any account is vitiated by our suspicion of its motives: what's behind this? Since nature cannot speak, human beings must speak on nature's behalf and perhaps even ventriloquize, so it looks as though nature is speaking after all. But all observation is based on pre-judgements that could as easily be different pre-judgements, and which cannot prove their own validity.

So observers have interests, and battle for power over the words to be used to describe the state of the environment. There's nothing to prevent the world ending while the battle over words and responsibility is still being waged. But nature doesn't ask to be described in a particular way. Nature doesn't care whether there's an interest behind every description of nature. And it doesn't care about the threat of destruction. It can change its state. It can become uninhabitable. But it cannot die.

Path 3: Responsibility

After the thousand conferences, a broad consensus has developed in the scientific world that CO_2 emissions have an aggregate effect on the climate of the earth. This raises the issue of who is responsible and what should be done. The problem with this is that no single actor has any direct responsibility. There is no simple chain of causes and effects events leading from me driving my car to the undoing of nature. And at all events my contribution is so small that it is unlikely to make a difference by itself. In fact the overall situation is so ungraspable that it seems reasonable to talk about 'non-knowledge', which makes it irresponsible to speak of responsibility at all.[6]

Although the inhabitants of the affluent world know that they are part of the problem, whether they are concerned or indifferent, they do not act together, and individually they only have a microscopic responsibility. They live separately in their individual houses or apartments. So who's to blame for the state of the planet?

Diffuse actors

In the absence of specific addresses where the responsibility can be placed, diffuse actors like 'the affluent world', 'industry' or 'the consumers' are constructed. Such actors are not self-evident. They are constructed by science, by the mass media and by politicians. But neither science nor the mass media acknowledge any responsibility. They see their role as that of the postman, the messenger. Industry too passes the buck on to the consumers. And so the monkey lands on the shoulders of the politicians.

The political market
It's easy to blame the politicians. But if you look closer, the politicians are in the same boat as industry. They too are part of a market with supply and demand where they are just as dependent on their voters as industry is on its customers. They cannot run faster into the future than the voters want. So if the voters want to preserve and improve their everyday life, only politicians with a strange death-wish will demand strict loyalty to the state of the planet.

The political struggle is about power and stands between government and opposition. In this game the environment is a single piece, so consideration of the environment is weighed against other considerations. The environment doesn't come up trumps. It only sets the agenda if the voters are worried. Claims about the state of the environment are judged not on their truth value, but on their capacity to influence and motivate voters.

There are ecological systems. But they have no independent power to decide and act.[7] If you want to speak for the environment, you must ally yourself with actors who can set the agenda and make decisions. This launches you on a circuit where it's easy to get lost – is it the politicians, civil servants, editors or leaders of industry you have to influence? Or all of them at once. And how is it done?

Even though the issue of the environment has moved from the periphery of society to the centre, it's hard to locate the responsibility, because it all goes round in circles. The industrialists point at the consumers, who point at the politicians, who point at the voters, who point at the mass media, who...

You could call it double standards. But there is no definitive place where you can locate the responsibility, and at the same time there is a strong wish not to assume responsibility oneself. The people who, out of loyalty to the state of the planet, change their lives, are regarded with indulgent sympathy, that is if they are not considered irritants, killjoys demanding that we hold back, turn off and leave alone. The party-pooper is no hero of everyday life.

Even if it could be documented beyond all doubt

– but who defines this 'beyond'? – that the polar ice will melt and cause flooding, we may still doubt that this threat would be taken seriously enough to check the burning desire for growth and luxury.

Path 4: Action
In theory perhaps everyone would agree that someone should do something. But this is where we come up against the 'where to put the garbage dump' dilemma: everyone agrees, no one volunteers. The rich will refuse to change their habits – and they are rich enough to be arrogant. The poor don't think they should be the ones to make sacrifices. The old people think that, after a hard working life, they have deserved their comfort. The young are busy making their mark, and are well aware that lavish consumption is a strong card in the struggle for recognition. Each professional group thinks its contribution to the wellbeing of society is so significant that cutbacks are irresponsible, whether in research, education or health services. And members of the large middle class are strapped firmly into the life they have promised themselves and their families. They can't give up their car, their holiday home, their gadgets, their two annual trips abroad and their culinary arrangements.

When everyone is responsible for himself or herself, you have to look hard for those who are responsible for the totality. And once more it's the politicians who first spring to mind. They lay down the rules that apply to everyone in society, and therefore act as the representatives of society, while all the others only represent themselves or their workplace.

We have seen how the politicians' hands are tied by the voters. This problem has a further dimension. Politicians are not elected by the global community, but in a nation. So while the problems of the environment are global, its actors are local. Even when they enter into alliances and work together across boundaries, they are tied by invisible cords to their native country and its special situation.

So the problem and the solution are at different levels. It's quite conceivable that the actors in the global community will only see beyond national considerations and agree on action when it's too late to avoid predictable catastrophes. Perhaps it takes worse crises than the current financial crisis, which in theory gives states a unique chance to set the agenda and demand consideration for the environment. "You shouldn't waste a good crisis...". In its shadow things that are normally impossible can be realized.

Yet there are few signs that politicians will seize the chance. It's too risky. While the market is unaccountable, politicians are accountable for the decisions they make. If things go wrong, we all know who the culprits are. So it's better to let things slide, lubricating the economy with subsidies and tax cuts.

The image of sustainability

But isn't sustainability simply a matter of living differently – consuming less and more wisely, driving cars charged with wind power, building houses that are so well insulated that if you fart in October you have heating until April? The idea of creating CO_2-neutral environments is tempting to politicians and building contractors who would like to show initiative and benefit both the environment and themselves. You would have to be a dyed-in-the-wool pessimist not to feel enlivened by the idea "Yes, we can!".

But there's a bogeyman behind the door. Many companies would be delighted to jump on the green bandwagon as a way of ensuring their growth. They would like to build energy-neutral houses. But the goal is growth, and consideration of the environment is a means to an end. Behind those green drapes the old game goes on. And who says it benefits the environment that a detergent is ten time more sustainable, if that means you sell 50 per cent more of it? Energy-neutral houses must be something more than symbolic measures for futuristic architects who want to prove *that it can be done*. They must be something more than the sophisticated kind of luxury where exclusive prototypes conceal the fact that most construction goes on as before.

Conclusion

Economy and ecology make contradictory demands. With all the good will in the world it's hard to see how the two kinds of demands can be reconciled. Can everyone have a job without production becoming so huge that the environment is smashed to pieces? Can everyone in the world, including the billions in China and India and Brazil, attain a western standard of living without the planet turning red hot and the waters rising? Are there any alternatives to the image of luxury that is currently being cultivated with such fervent energy?

I'd like to be an optimist, but it's difficult. The mechanisms available to resolve the crisis are not adapted to the problems. National politicians, elected by local voters, must solve global problems together. That drags the problem into the quagmire of political negotiations. And everyone knows that once an issue is politicized, solutions are hard to see.

The short-term solution is probably that the contradictory demands must be handled in the time-honoured way: with hypocrisy, that is by disconnecting words and actions. You sing the praises of the environment, but at the same time you worship the idols of economics. And only because you go in for the environment in such a big way can you get away with systematically ignoring its demands.

1. Ole Thyssen, *Verdenssamfundet. Et filosofisk essay (The World Society. A Philosophical Essay)*, Copenhagen: Hans Reitzels Forlag, 2009, p. 50.
2. G.W.F. Hegel, *Philosophy of Right*, §§ 191 and 195.
3. Friedrich Nietzsche, *Således talte Zarathustra*. Copenhagen: Jespersens og Pios Forlag, 1934, p. 128.
4. I discussed this theme many years ago in *Den anden natur (Second Nature)*, Copenhagen: Vindrose, 1982.
5. Niklas Luhmann, *Beobachtungen der Moderne*, Opladen: Westdeutscher Verlag, 1992.
6. Niklas Luhmann, *Ökologie des Nicht-Wissens, Beobachtungen der Moderne*, Opladen: Westdeutscher Verlag, 1992.
7. Niklas Luhmann, *Ökologische Kommunikation*, Opladen: Westdeutscher Verlag, 1986.

Ole Thyssen is Dr.Phil in philosophy, Professor at the Department of Management, Politics and Philosophy at Copenhagen Business School and the author of a number of books on social philosophy, ethics and aesthetics.

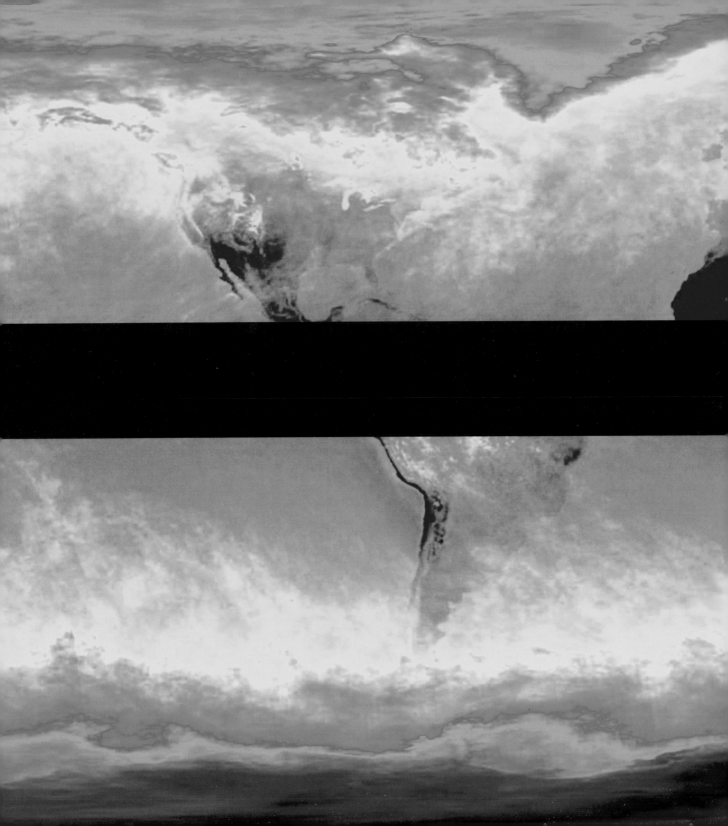

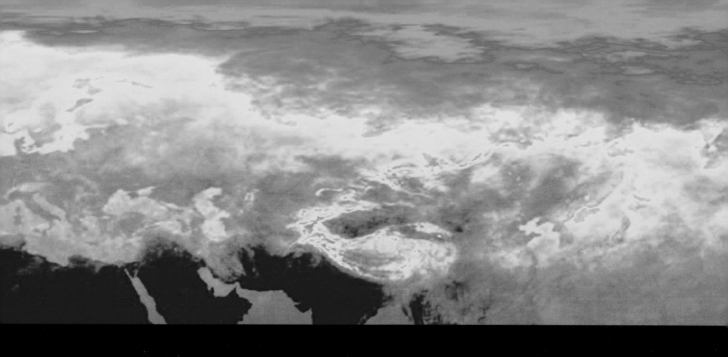

CLIMATE

FIH Bank Headquarters

Copenhagen, 2008
Sauerbruch Hutton, Berlin

The new FIH Bank headquarters at Langelinie is part of an overall urban transformation of the old quay areas Marmormolen and Nordhavn into a sustainable city.

The curved ends of the volume permit maximum orientation towards the water on both sides of the site. The double-layer glass façade enables maximum transparency while minimizing thermal disadvantages. The space between the glass layers acts as a thermal buffer, as a solar collector and as a protective layer for efficient shading. Rotating and sliding lamellae offer full protection against overheating and glare.

The surrounding water reflects sunlight and forms a basis for optimizing daylight inside the building through extensive façade glazing and an atrium in the centre part of the building. As a result, artificial lighting can be reduced to a minimum.

As a contemporary office building, the server room creates excess heat that can be used to warm up the building in the winter period and to produce the necessary cooling for the server room itself. Sea water can supply the required energy by conducting it through the building, i.e. through thermo-active slabs, which means that the building mass itself is used to supply thermal comfort. The entire hot water requirement can be met by tapping into the return heat from the district heating system.

Natural ventilation is possible through the double-layer glazing system. The inner façade opens up freely to permit air exchange, while the outer layer absorbs wind load and protects the solar shading devices positioned in between the two layers. The space between the two facades also functions as a thermal buffer.

The large 'flying roof' on top of the building could be made of a technical textile. The roof traps and channels the westerly winds to run a series of silent wind turbines producing electricity. These are placed horizontally between the penthouse and the wing-shaped roof. Another source of energy is the sun, through photovoltaic panels integrated in the tilted outer glazing of the façade.

Combining an integrated environmental concept and contemporary technology, the project thus maximizes both comfort and energy efficiency in a new aesthetic. The overall colour scheme matches the hues of the surrounding warehouses, giving the building an endlessly changing appearance.

01 electricity production by wind turbines
02 canopy roof maximizes efficiency of wind turbines
03 sea water used to cool the building
04 photovoltaics integrated in roof and facade
05 choice of materials based on environmental product declarations
06 collection and re-use of rainwater
07 excess heat recovery from server room
08 enhanced night cooling using thermal mass of the primary construction
09 integrated and wind protected solar shading
10 double layered facade for thermal and sound insulation
11 thermally activated slabs
12 passive solar considerations
13 high level of air tightness
14 high thermal insulation

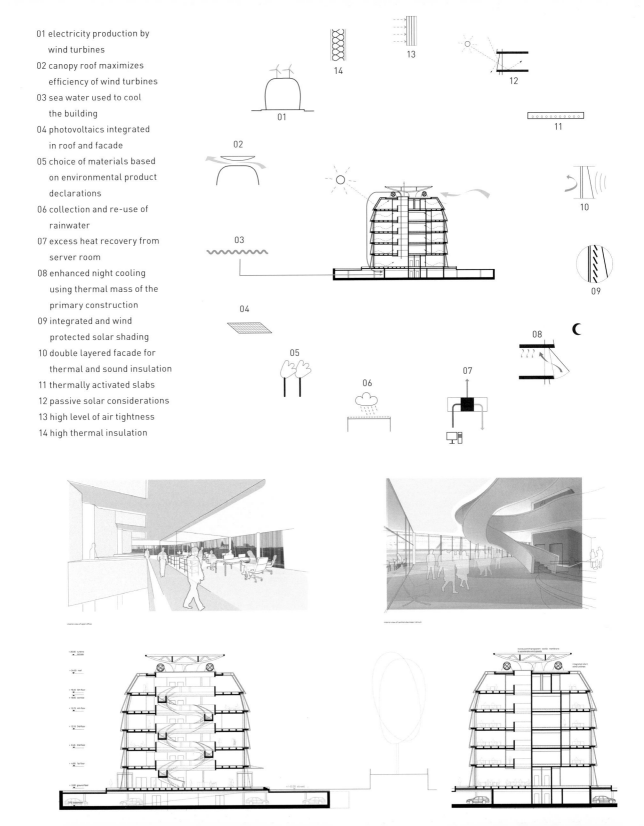

SIEEB

Beijing, 2003 - 2006
Mario Cucinella Architects, Paris og Bologne

**Sino-Italian Ecological and
Energy-Efficient Building**
This project is a joint venture of the Italian and
Chinese Governments. It involves a new 20,000
m² faculty building at Tsinghua University which
houses a Sino-Italian education, training and
research centre for environmental protection and
energy conservation. The building is designed as
a showcase for the potential reduction of CO_2-
emissions in China. The design integrates passive
and active strategies to control the external environment in order to optimize internal environmental conditions. The building is U-shaped in
plan around a central courtyard, and on the
ground floor public areas look out over a landscaped garden. It is closed and well insulated on
the northern side, which faces the cold winter
winds, and open and transparent towards the
south. Offices and laboratories on the upper
floors have terraced gardens shaded by photovoltaic panels that produce energy for the building. The solar panels appear as an integral part of
the architecture and thus help to create the form
of the building. SIEEB is an example of how new
types of energy can contribute to the aesthetics of
the architecture of the future.

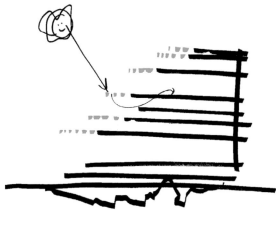

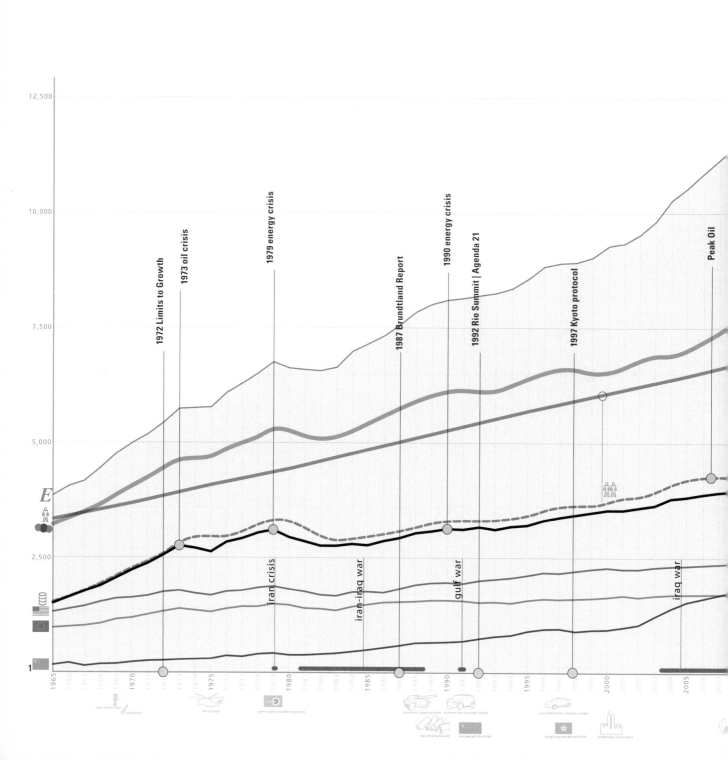

12,500

10,000

7,500

5,000

E

2,500

1972 Limits to Growth

1973 oil crisis

1979 energy crisis

1987 Brundtland Report

1990 energy crisis

1992 Rio Summit | Agenda 21

1997 Kyoto protocol

Peak Oil

iran crisis

iran-iraq war

gulf war

iraq war

1

1965 · 1966 · 1967 · 1968 · 1969 · 1970 · 1971 · 1972 · 1973 · 1974 · 1975 · 1976 · 1977 · 1978 · 1979 · 1980 · 1981 · 1982 · 1983 · 1984 · 1985 · 1986 · 1987 · 1988 · 1989 · 1990 · 1991 · 1992 · 1993 · 1994 · 1995 · 1996 · 1997 · 1998 · 1999 · 2000 · 2001 · 2002 · 2003 · 2004 · 2005 · 2006 · 2007

man on the moon · woodstock · fall of saigon · greens party founded in germany · tiananmen square protests · toyota hits consumer market · prius hybrid hits consumer market · fall of the berlin wall · warsaw pact dissolved · hong kong transferred to PRC · world trade centre attack

Transsolar
Climate Engineering

residential

transportation

buildings

industry

E/sector typical western nation
survey 2004

E/👤 survey 2000

kgoe

8000
7000
6000
5000
4000
3000
2000
1000
0

world average

2015   2020   2025   2030

E **Total World Energy Consumption (Mtoe)**

Mtoe = energy value = million tonnes of oil equivalent
1 tonne of oil = 318 gallons, or 1,204 litres gasoline
11.6 MW hours electricity

Total World Primary Energy Consumption
US Total Primary Energy Consumption
EU Total Primary Enrgy Consumption
China Total Primary Energy Consumption

Total World Oil Consumption (Mtoe)

Total World Oil Consumption
Predicted Oil Resources

Global Carbon Fossil Emissions (metric tonnes)

👤 **Total World Population (millions)**

E/👤 **Energy Use per Capita (kgoe)**

kgoe = kilograms of oil equivalent
1 kgoe = 1/3 US gallons
1.2 litres gasoline
11.6 kW hours electricity

Sources include: BP Statistical Review of World Energy 2006:
EarthMatters 2000, Columbia Earth Institute
Energy Information Administration
UN Economic and Social Affairs/Population Division
World Resources Institute: EarthTrends,
Environmental Information
wikipedia.org

Climate engineering seeks to improve the built environment's impact on the environment while maintaining the highest indoor and outdoor comfort. Transsolar accomplishes this by developing and validating innovative climate and energy concepts. Transsolar works collaboratively with clients, architects, mechanical engineers, and other consultants from the earliest stages of the building design process, considering each step from the standpoint of fundamental thermodynamics and physics. This generates a solution in which local conditions, form, material, and mechanical systems are integrated components of a well-orchestrated climate control system which reduces operating costs while increasing occupant comfort.

Transsolar work considers more than energy conservation based upon optimizing thermal properties of the building envelope and efficiency of technical equipment. In addition, they seek a more holistic design recognizing the interdependence of factors affecting comfort and integrating the functions of architectural and technical equipment. Transsolar addresses DAYLIGHT, NATURAL VENTILATION, AIR QUALITY, AIR TEMPERATURE, ACOUSTICS, and THE WELL-BEING OF PEOPLE.

Founded in Germany in 1992, today Transsolar is working on projects worldwide with forty engineers in New York, Stuttgart, and Munich. We enjoy the discovery process of responding to new climatic conditions, new design partners, and new user demands. In all cases, though, the aims are the same: comfortable, ecological, economical, and high-value buildings and urban environments for living and working.

71

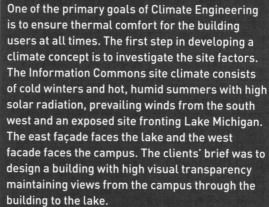

TEMPERATURE – COMFORT

Richard J. Klarchek Information Commons

Chicago, 2008
Solomon Cordwell Buenz, Chicago

One of the primary goals of Climate Engineering is to ensure thermal comfort for the building users at all times. The first step in developing a climate concept is to investigate the site factors. The Information Commons site climate consists of cold winters and hot, humid summers with high solar radiation, prevailing winds from the south west and an exposed site fronting Lake Michigan. The east façade faces the lake and the west facade faces the campus. The clients' brief was to design a building with high visual transparency maintaining views from the campus through the building to the lake.

This indicated that a façade with integrated, automatic shading devices was needed to mitigate heat gains from the rising and setting sun on the fully glazed east and west elevations. In addition, precast slab-embedded radiant heating and cooling provide the bulk of active temperature control. Underfloor displacement ventilation provides fresh air and dehumidification. The sum of these measures achieves a highly comfortable space while maintaining a high- glazed, transparent effect.

AIR – NATURAL VENTILATION

KfW Banking Group

Frankfurt, 2009
Sauerbruch Hutton Generalplanungsgesells-
chaft mbH, Berlin

In high-rise buildings wind pressures on the facade must be analysed not only for structural design, but also for the impact on the natural ventilation of the offices.

In the 15-storey addition to the KfW Banking Group's headquarters in Frankfurt a double-layered wind-pressurized façade offers natural ventilation independent of external conditions. The design and active control of the façade guarantees ventilation from the façade via operable windows while limiting unwanted cross-ventilation and draft between the offices.

Manitoba Hydro Headquarters

Winnipeg, 2008
Sauerbruch Hutton Generalplanungsgesells-
chaft mbH, Berlin

The strength, direction and relative frequency of winds is essential in the design and layout of buildings to assure pedestrian comfort, good city ventilation patterns and reduced energy consumption.

For the Manitoba Hydro Headquarter in Winnipeg the prevailing southerly winds drive natural ventilation through the south-facing winter garden. The primary facades, however, are parallel to this wind and therefore require an additional driving force for natural ventilation. A solar thermal chimney uses the natural buoyancy of warm air to pull air through these facades. Since the air is not conditioned, it can enter through large openings in the facade rather than the restrictive heating coil, cooling coil, or heat exchanger in an air handling unit. Thus air movement requires much less power, so that the small pressure differences generated by the solar chimney are sufficient.

SOUND – AMBIENCE

Norddeutsche Landesbank,

Hanover, 2002
Behnisch, Behnisch & Partner / Behnisch
Architekten, Stuttgart

The Norddeutsche Landesbank is located in the
Hanover city centre, adjacent to egidientorplatz,
to the northeast, and Friedrichswall, both
adversely affected by heavy traffic.

From the exterior, the building complex resem-
bles a traditional city block, but at its centre, protected from the noise of the surrounding streets,
lies an 'oasis' – a large, new courtyard.

The building has a double façade with multiple
benefits, providing protection against noise and
vehicle emissions, lending wind protection to the
external blind systems (thereby increasing their
effectiveness), and serving as a supply air duct to
adjacent offices. By introducing the 'clean' air
from the beneficial microclimate of the courtyard
into the void of the double façade, it is possible to
achieve window ventilation even on those sides of
the building exposed to noisy street traffic. All
rooms can thereby be ventilated naturally
through simple window openings and by exploit-
ing the cooling potential of outdoor air, which
exceeds 22°C during less than five per cent of the
year.

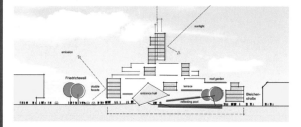

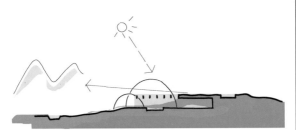

Bad Aibling Spa Baths

Bad Aibling, 2007
Behnisch Architekten, Stuttgart

The optimization of daylight use during the design process led from the original fully glazed roof to a new design, with only 8% glazing or openings. The hall and the domes now have the highest possible daylight quality and carefully differentiated qualities of light. The relaxation zones receive normal daylight with a fully lit sun deck in winter, shaded by leaves in summer. The daylight level throughout the hall is high, with transparent and translucent openings to ensure optimum visual connections and light diffusion. Ring-shaped skylights accentuate the shape of the domes and individual light concepts enhance the distinct character of each dome interior.

Simulation tools were used to plot the diffusion and patterns of light throughout the hall and domes. This analysis, together with photo-realistic visualizations of all areas, informed and supported the decision-making process.

MATERIAL – MASS VERSUS MEMBRANE

Suvarnabhumi Airport

Bangkok, 2005
Murphy/Jahn, Chicago

Lightweight materials such as membranes provide the ability to create tailor-made indoor environments. The new international airport in Bangkok is one of the largest airports in the world. When the outdoor temperature is 35°C (95°F), when the airport terminal is filled with heat-producing electrical equipment, and when vast numbers of people pass through the building around the clock, the design of a comfortable indoor environment requires special solutions.

The result developed is a triple-layer membrane system which spans the entire 3.5 km long concourse. This allows a lightweight material, easily capable of spanning the concourse width, to still achieve a variety of thermal, acoustic and daylighting functions. The outer membrane is a PTFE-coated glass fibre composite, distinguished by high reflectivity, tensile strength, dirt repellence and durability. The middle layer, 6 mm transparent polycarbonate sheets attached to a steel cable mesh, serves primarily as sound protection. The inner layer of the system, which has a low-emissivity coating on the interior side, is an open-weave glass-fibre material that allows the interior noise to pass through to the middle layer. The membrane combines excellent low-emissivity (low emittance of heat radiation) and acoustic absorption properties in addition to translucence.

Linked Hybrid

Beijing, 2008
Steven Holl Architects, New York

The differing physical aspects of various materials have a distinct impact on the environmental quality of a space. Exposed thermal mass, such as concrete structural elements, mitigates the amplitude of indoor temperature changes by storing heat during the day and discharging it through night air flushing. Hydronic piping within the concrete can enhance this thermal activation process.

Linked Hybrid's thermal building mass is activated via slab-integrated radiant piping systems, ensuring thermal comfort within the apartments and using the free cooling potential of a geothermal energy system. The ground-source heat-pump system is one of the largest residential systems in the world and shoulders 70% of the complex's yearly heating and cooling load. The system is comprised of 660 geothermal wells penetrating 100 metres below the basement foundation, providing a total 5000 kW cooling and heating capacity.

HUMAN SCALE

Lycée Charles de Gaulle

Damascus, 2008
Ateliers Lion architectes urbanistes, Paris

Each building site has its own general climate, microclimate, specific boundaries and local resources which must be explored. For the new French School in Damascus, Transsolar was asked to work with the architects Ateliers Lion to develop a climate concept attuned to the local climate conditions.

The school complex is made up of small buildings, each with two stacked classrooms, connected via small courtyards. The goal was to find a low-technology solution for ventilation and conditioning of the rooms using local materials as a modern interpretation of the traditional architecture. Syria has a dry desert climate with hot days and cold nights. This local climate situation was analysed and the concept of wind-assisted solar chimneys used to drive natural cross-ventilation through the classrooms was developed to provide thermal comfort without any mechanical support. Combined with the shaded, vegetated courtyards, the overall affect is an exceptionally positive human experience relying on simple technologies.

RiverPark Development

Pittsburgh, 2006-2014
Behnisch Architekten, Stuttgart

RiverPark will have its own unique character. Each residential block will have a distinct identity which respects the human scale, provides individual addresses, and contributes to a much improved public realm.

For RiverPark to become a lively, integral part of Pittsburgh, it is important to understand and respond to the demands of various potential user groups. A public life analysis provided information on where people walk and spend time either as part of their daily activities or for recreational purposes. The end result is that each neighbourhood is uniquely expressed as an "urban living room" offering a wide range of opportunities for people of all ages to enjoy downtown living.

To maximize the use of these outdoor spaces, a comfortable outdoor climate should be maintained by passive means in nearly all weather conditions. In winter, this requires shelter from the wind and exposure to the sun. Building mass is structured to buffer the cold westerly winds, in addition to staggered building heights to allow ample sunlight at ground level in the middle of the day.

Combined with the extensive re-use of existing buildings, the creation of such a liveable, yet dense urban environment is highly sustainable.

New Vernacular

One of the most important requirements of sustainable architecture is that it must relate adaptively to the place where it is built. Considerations of climate, the materials that exist in the area and the consumption of resources are all crucial. Allowances can be made for the local wind conditions, so that each side of a building can be given its own formal expression. Traditional regional architecture is often designed in accordance with its own climatic zone, and over time architects have been inspired by indigenous building customs – technologically, aesthetically and in their choice of materials.

1. Turf-built house, Iceland.
The house is exposed without any shelter from wind and water. So it is built down on terrain where one can exploit the ability of the earth to absorb damp and heat. Walls and roofs are of grass and turf, and inside the house is clad with wood that retains heat. Subarctic climate.

2. Mud house, Syria, subtropical climate.
The Syrian 'beehive house' is actually an imitation of earth dugouts that delay the extreme temperature fluctuations between day and night that occur in the desert. It is built of packed earthen walls with small openings that shelter the occupants from the extremely harsh light and the heat. The tall vaulted construction is built of mud-packed stones and straw. Beehive houses are used both as homes and for storage of things like food that need to be kept cool in the hot conditions.

3. Sámi tent, Lapland, subarctic climate.
The tents of the Sámi are nomadic dwellings. They are heated by the fireplace in the middle of the tent with a smoke-opening at the top.

4. Yurt, Mongolia, Arctic climate.
The yurt is a kind of nomadic dwelling, more sophisticated than the tents. In these too the fireplace is the central element in the dwelling, which is typically insulated with animal skins.

5. Iglo. Greenland, arctic climate.
This kind of dwelling exploits the available material in extremely cold areas: the blocks of snow contain air and therefore have an insulating effect. The hemispherical shape of the igloo gives it a minimum surface area compared to its volume, and the reinforced entrance section counteracts further heat loss. Arctic climate.

6. Straw hut, Central Africa, tropical climate.
Huts made of straw are temporary homes for nomadic herders. The are easy to build and take down again. The herd is moved with the changing seasons between mountain and lowland pastures, and the hut is an example of considerate exploitation of natural resources.

7. Houses on posts, Malaysia, tropical climate.
Houses on posts, built in light materials that exploit the wind and ventilation. At the same time the space beneath the house protects the occupants from damp, flooding and animal pests. Houses on posts are mainly found in the subtropical climatic zone, where there is a lot of rainfall and high humidity.

8. Cave houses, Canary Islands, subtropical climate.
Cave houses are highly energy-efficient, since with their basis in a mountain face they need far less cooling and heating. The temperature in these homes is more or less constant all year round, and they balance out the temperature fluctuations of the day: at night the stone has absorbed heat from the sun, while during they day they retain their coolness longer than the surroundings.

The Moving School

Goa, 2001–
Mette Lange and Anders Linnet

The Moving School is a project that takes its point of departure in the economic and social conditions in the southern Indian state of Goa. The fast-growing construction sector requires a mobile workforce from among the poorest, unskilled part of the population, people who are willing to move between localities and regions. The children of these families form a particularly vulnerable group who are prevented from getting a basic education by the linguistic differences between the states and the temporary character of the work. The Moving School concept follows the schoolchildren, ensuring teaching in their own language and thus a better start in life. The intention is to develop the concept further for free use in other areas of the world.

The movable school units are built with available materials and in accordance with traditional building principles that can be used by ordinary craftsmen and workers wherever there is a need. The 'floating school' is like a raft with a bamboo hut, while the 'rolling school' is like an agricultural trailer that can be driven by a vehicle to its destination. The materials are mainly bamboo and metal, which are available all over India. The construction is flexible and spacious: walls can be folded out and become roofs, increasing the floor area, and gables have storage space for blackboards and desks for the teachers. At the same time the materials and construction ensure light and ventilation, while insulating against excessive heat and monsoon rain. A solar heating unit on the roof provides electricity so that teaching can also take place in the evening.

The project has mainly been financed by fundraising in Denmark and is run by an Indian NGO, www.movingschool.org.

All the work is voluntary, and all donations go in their entirety to the school units in India.

The METI School in Bangladesh

Bangladesh, 2005
Anna Heringer and Eike Roswag

The METI School facilitates the use of individual, free teaching techniques and improves the quality of life and development in buildings in rural areas at low cost, using locally available resources by disseminating and developing knowledge among the local population.

On the ground floor with its thick clay walls there are three classrooms, each with its own exit to an organically designed system af 'caves' behind the classroom.

The upper floor, which is built with bamboo, is by contrast light and open and offers a magnificent view of the surroundings, while its large interior offers plenty of space for movement. The use of clay and bamboo as building materials draws on traditional construction techniques with technical improvements, demonstrating how locally available resources, skills and manpower can be used to build better, more cost-effective buildings. Twenty-five workers from the close local neighbourhood of the school were trained in the new techniques and participated in the construction of the building. Similarly, schoolchildren and teachers were integrated throughout the building process and contributed to the building of their own school by making objects like rolls of straw and clay for the door and window frames.

The school was built for and in collaboration with the Modern Education and Training Institute (METI) and the main NGO Dipshikha in 2005 at Rudrapur in northern Bangladesh. The project was implemented in cooperation with the voluntary association Shanti Bangladesch and the Papal Mission for Children (PMK).

Ecological movements

Arcosanti, Järna and Thorup

The ecological and environmental movements of the 1960s and 1970s concerned themselves with renewable energy and natural resources as a totality – from food to buildings and occupations. The fundamental social idea of shared responsibility became the starting-point for several mini-societies.

Torup

The 'eco-village' Dyssekilde in Torup was founded in 1989 with the aim of creating a spiritual community based on love and responsibility towards human beings, animals, plants, the environment and resources. The village consists of five dwelling groups, a kindergarten, school, a meeting house, a shop, small firms and a wind turbine. Some houses were designed by architects, others by the occupants themselves; all of them were built with a focus on recyclable materials, minimum material consumption or heat emissions. Among other things, the 'Earth Dome' was positioned in accordance with the earth's axis and covered with earth that functions as a heat store.

Järna

Järna is an ecological urban community about 50 km from Stockholm in Sweden. The small community is based on anthroposophical ideas: mankind is spiritually linked nature and the cosmos. Rudolf Steiner's ideas on education, learning, art, architecture and organic farming form the basis for the Järna community, which besides homes, a cultural centre and a school also has the only anthroposophical hospital in Scandinavia. Parts of the community were designed by the Danish architect Erik Asmussen. The houses, in accordance with the local Swedish customs, are pastel-coloured or in strong, clear colours. Despite the esoteric associations, the houses adhere to a fundamentally functionalist attitude and are adapted individually to the needs of the users.

Arcosanti

Arcosanti is an experimental community in the Arizona Desert, founded in 1970. When fully developed, the town will house 5000 people in an urban lifestyle free of some of the problems that haunt big cities. The town is based on the Italian architect Paolo Soleri's concept 'arcology' (architecture + ecology). The greenhouse is a kind of solar cell for the town in the winter, since the heated air rises up the slope and heats the town. In summer the wind from the plain cools the buildings down. The town also draws local inspiration from the Hopi Indians' traditional exploitation of the shadow formations in the ravine.

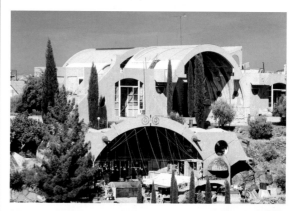

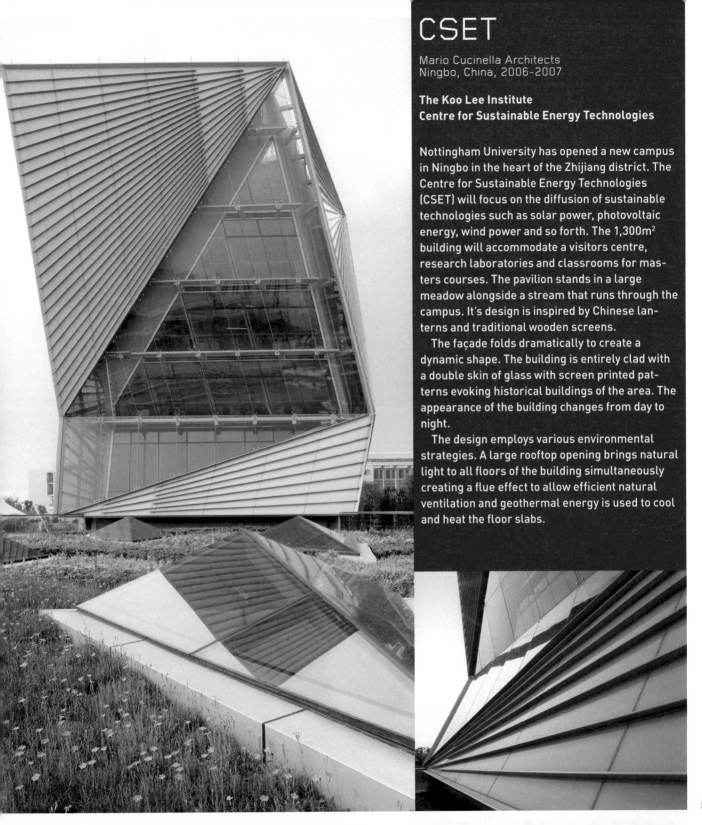

CSET

Mario Cucinella Architects
Ningbo, China, 2006-2007

**The Koo Lee Institute
Centre for Sustainable Energy Technologies**

Nottingham University has opened a new campus in Ningbo in the heart of the Zhijiang district. The Centre for Sustainable Energy Technologies (CSET) will focus on the diffusion of sustainable technologies such as solar power, photovoltaic energy, wind power and so forth. The 1,300m² building will accommodate a visitors centre, research laboratories and classrooms for masters courses. The pavilion stands in a large meadow alongside a stream that runs through the campus. It's design is inspired by Chinese lanterns and traditional wooden screens.

The façade folds dramatically to create a dynamic shape. The building is entirely clad with a double skin of glass with screen printed patterns evoking historical buildings of the area. The appearance of the building changes from day to night.

The design employs various environmental strategies. A large rooftop opening brings natural light to all floors of the building simultaneously creating a flue effect to allow efficient natural ventilation and geothermal energy is used to cool and heat the floor slabs.

The Water Cube

The National Swimming Centre (Water Cube)
for the Beijing Olympic Games 2008
PTW Architects with China State Construction
Design (CCDI) and ARUP

The Water Cube associates water as a structural and conceptual Leitmotiv with the square, the primal shape of the house in Chinese tradition and mythology. The structure of the Water Cube is based on a unique lightweight construction developed by China State Construction Design (CCDI), PTW Architects & ARUP, and is derived from the structure of water bubbles in the state of aggregation found in foam. Their transparency and apparent randomness is reflected in the inner and outer 'skins' of the building, in a system made of inflated EFTE cushions. The architectural space, structure and facade of the Water Cube are built with the same kind of element.

The design makes use of natural sunlight, harnessing solar energy to heat the building and the water. Water will be conserved by means of rainwater harvesting and water-efficient systems. The design uses the latest technology and materials to create a visually striking, energy-efficient and environment-friendly building.

Cladding the building with high-tech EFTE cushions, which have excellent insulation properties, will create a greenhouse effect, harnessing the power of the sun to heat the interior of the building and the pool water.

As water in northern China is a valuable commodity, and Beijing currently lacks a reliable water resource, water-sensitive urban design principles are being incorporated. In this way water is reused and recycled after being collected in roof catchment areas, pool backwash systems and overland flows.

The New Monte Rosa Hut

Zermatt
ETH, Zürich

The Swiss Alpine Club's New Monte Rosa Hut is in a mountain landscape with extreme climatic conditions far from the supply network of civilization. This applies to everything to do with production, logistics at the construction site, the self-sufficient infrastructure and the operation of the hut. The project is a five-storey polygonal building – a prefabricated wood construction where the wood has been turned with traditional building methods in a computer-aided process. This mechanical production method enables the use of traditional craftsmanship methods such as half-timbering with its geometrically complex wood joints.

The high-insulation metallic facade is clad with solar-cell panels that supply the building with the necessary operating energy for purifying waste water, ventilation, lighting and electrical installations (90% self-sufficient). Excess energy is received and stored in batteries. A stairway follows a window band that traces the course of the sun around the building and conducts passive energy into the dining hall, winds like a spiral around the whole building and makes it possible to enjoy the view on all sides.

The Monte Rosa Hut includes a restaurant and overnight accommodation for 120 guests.

It is expected that the project will be completed in the autumn of 2009.

LAB III

Astronomy in the home

Philippe Rahm Architects

Atmospheric home

The atmospheric home is the prototype of an apartment where you no longer occupy a surface, you occupy an atmosphere. As they leave the floor, the functions and furnishings rise: they spread and evaporate in the atmosphere of the apartment, and they stabilize at certain temperatures determined by the body, clothing and activity.

Our proposal is to make allowances for these physical differences in the distribution of temperature in the space and to exploit them by changing the way we live; to replace a horizontal way of living with a vertical one where we can occupy different heat zones, different layers, different heights. And thus to create a global ecosystem like a kind of astronomy of the home, where combinations of temperature, light, time and place are reconfigured.

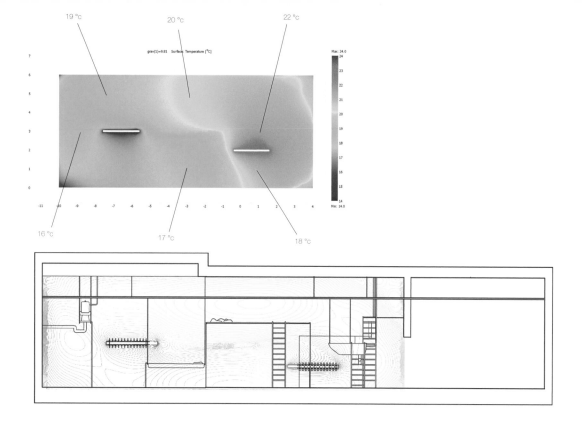

Philippe Rahm Architects
Interview with Philippe Rahm

By Peter Andreas Sattrup

PAS: What are the issues you explore in your work?
PR: Architecture's challenges and its field are related to space, time, seasons, climate and atmosphere. Right at the beginning of architecture you have this goal – to change the climate, to lengthen the day in relation to the night by lighting candles. When you build a hut in the Finland winter it's with a view to recreating or keeping a little bit of spring or summer. You could also say that architecture has a wish to recreate the Garden of Eden, where you could walk around naked and live without architecture. After the Deluge, if I may express myself symbolically, the need for architecture arises – to make this little change in the climate that the building represents. I think this is the most

important, fundamental idea in architecture: to define a new climate in relation to the climate outside. It may be that the people and architects of former times didn't have such good tools to change the cycle of day and night, the astronomical cycle: a candle, a fireplace. But at the beginning of the nineteenth century new and stronger tools were introduced. It started with gaslight. The moment in 1812 when London got street lighting, we began to create a kind of eternal day in the city, and to depart from the natural cycle. The next stage of development was the development of heating systems, the radiator and central heating. With Frank Lloyd Wright you see these systems integrated in architecture. Le Corbusier's mur neutralisant also has this function, to create a regular temperature around 18°C, and set it up as a universal ideal. It's this development in man-made climate changes that starts with modernity and leads to our situation today.

So you think that the climatic starting-point for architecture is much more important than the communicative one?
Yes, I'm not really interested in signs, symbolism or narratives. Heidegger was against the idea of a standardized indoor climate, and argued that you had to respect the changes in the day and the seasons. But in time this distortion of time and the seasons has become all the more marked, and is now worldwide and has led to the global warming we see now. Our means of communication too, the telephone and the Internet, help to reinforce this distortion. The philosopher Peter Sloterdijk says that there is no longer an outside – the whole planet is now an inside. Before, we heated the interior of the house, but now we are also in the process of heating its exterior. We have to understand that we are living in an artificial world.

So the wish to recreate Paradise indoors has been transformed into a wish for control, resulting in a standardized indoor climate norm, the so-called comfort zone between 18 and 24°C, with the result that people have become alienated from the natural climate?
Precisely. I don't want to do the same in my work. Here where we sit, it's 20°. When you take a taxi it's 20°. Even if it's snowing in Paris today, it's 20° in the airport, and in the plane. When you come to Copenhagen, it will be 20° in your home. There's a continuum of 20° everywhere on the planet. In places like Dubai, too, for example, we are experiencing a normalization or even a banalization of the climate. There's an interesting relationship between symmetry and asymmetry. If you read Vitruvius or Alberti, symmetry is the aesthetic ideal for architecture. With the urban plans of the twentieth century and Frank Lloyd Wright's architecture, asymmetry becomes a new ideal, which becomes more and more pronounced, for example in the architecture of Deconstructivism. But at the same time as asymmetry becomes more and more dominant in the visible, the invisible, the indoor climate, becomes more and more symmetrical. With air-conditioning you try to cancel out the asymmetry and create an even temperature distribution throughout the space, a symmetry.

Why is architectural development lagging behind in the matter of the indoor climate?
There's a classic opposition between man and nature. For Hegel aesthetics is a matter of cultivating the natural, of domesticating the wilderness. You can also see French garden art as an expression of the wish to plant a mental order in the landscape. It's as if, with the increasing control of the indoor climate, no one was interested in affirming the invisible in the field of the visible, only in using our energies to develop form more freely.

But that oblivion to which much of the architecture of the past fifty years has consigned the climate – is it to do with the fact that the indoor climate is considered more to be an engineering issue, a question of technology rather than architecture?
Yes, but it's also a matter of the conception of empty space. Very late in the evolution of mankind we realized that the space between us is not empty. Louis Pasteur discovered that the air is full of microscopic life. But the great majority of the books you read as an architect are about the visible, not the invisible. I think we need to understand this situation. As architects we no longer work only with the visible, but also with the invisible, with the climate, with time, with the seasons. Climate, meteorology and time are the most important elements in my work. I don't want to get into a modernist, normalized banalization of this, I don't want 20° everywhere. I want to open up. It's a little like early modernism, which could contain both a Functionalism and le Corbusier's open plan, which is a showdown with the closed spaces and creates this freedom to move through space. For me it's a question of creating an open climatic landscape. I think of the building as an open climate, as an atmosphere. The issue of the climate also becomes a tool for creating architecture, if you consider the new technologies for creating low-energy buildings and for reducing the emissions of greenhouse gases. Creating more sustainable buildings is more about the invisible than the visible, and is linked with a climatic understanding of architecture. Materials are not as important as the energy used on heating and hot water. Buildings use up to 50% of the total energy in Switzerland. In order to reduce energy

consumption by a factor of eight and decrease heat loss they insulate in Switzerland with up to 40 cm of mineral wool and seal the houses so you can heat your room with a single candle. But then you also need to renew the air, since you consume the oxygen and give off a lot of moisture. When the building is insulated this way, the need arises to create a new climate indoors, since it's completely separated from the outside climate. So all these issues – the distortion of time and space, climatic changes and the technology we use to reduce energy consumption in our buildings – are the basis for my view that architecture is becoming meteorology.

So the need arises to create an artificial but qualitative environment on the basis of low-energy technology. Is it necessary to accept this artificiality, instead of "going back to nature"? Do you accept this artificiality?
Yes, it's a paradox. When you think about the perception of ecological building, it was precisely something to do with wood, contact with nature etc. But the most sustainable construction now is super-insulated and creates its own artificial climate. If you open the window you lose energy. That is really a paradox. For some people it's unacceptable, but I accept it. If you accept technology you also discover that you can create a basis for new design and new typologies. The traditional typology for apartments built up around a corridor, for example, reflects a bourgeois set of values from the nineteenth century. But what will the form of the home be like if you instead take the latest climatic technology as your point of departure? We drew up a project that was built up around the spatial flow of temperature and relative humidity in a home. The air from the outside is conducted in to the driest room in the home, the bedroom. While you sleep, you emit a good deal of moisture that is transported by the air. The air from here is drawn on through living room, kitchen and bathroom, where the humidity of the air constantly rises. You could say that an artificial wind blows through the house, related to the need for air exchange.

That thought comes very close to the ventilation diagram in the passive house concept for low-energy building. You could start a project with the ventilation diagram?
 – Yes, instead of beginning with a bourgeois social diagram, or a postmodernist stylistic reference. It is

a passive house concept, built up around heat recovery via mechanical ventilation. I think it's a very interesting diagram, which points to some great challenges. One of the most important things today is to work with the movements of the air. It's just like when the Greeks began to work with stone, and discovered that the material could be modulated, or when people later began to work with steel and saw the new structural possibilities the material offered. Or concrete, which offered new plasticity and a new aesthetic. We can do the same with the new technology. I think it's interesting to follow the movements of the air and to work with the invisible. Working with humidity, for example, creates an atmospheric landscape that also has a lot of sensory potential. The body has a relationship with the space. That also changes our view of the space, and perhaps our way of organizing it as a typology. Maybe we don't need categories like bedroom, bathroom, kitchen etc. Instead we can talk about dry rooms, medium-dry rooms or moist rooms. Perhaps we don't even need to separate then. In one project we have a kitchen-bathroom-living room. The function becomes fluid. You see it in traditional architecture too. In the old houses in Baghdad the names of the rooms refer to their climatic qualities, not to their use. In the evening the living room is perhaps by the patio, because it's cool at that time, in the daytime it may be in the basement. The function migrates with the diurnal rhythm.

It isn't far from the traditional Japanese house either, where you unfold the function with the furnishings, and the rooms change their programme with the family's daily social rhythm?
Yes, exactly. We have done several projects that work with this idea – for example a new national museum in Estonia, a school in Switzerland and a sports centre in Lyons. In all these projects there are invisible parameters – the heat, the relative air humidity, the light and the air exchange – underlying the design, in a highly calculated way. That gave me a desire to introduce an asymmetry, a new kind of disorder. My installation for the Biennale in Venice last year was actually the prototype for a home I am designing for Dominique Gonzales-Foerster. We know from Archimedes that warm air rises and cold air falls. In a normal home with radiators the warm air will have a tendency to gather up under the ceiling without doing any good despite all the energy

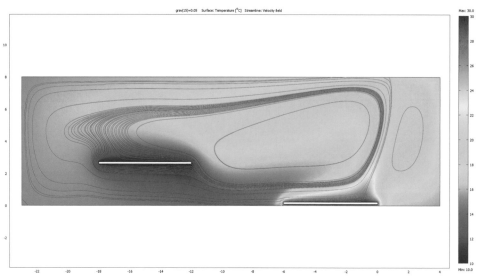

grav(15)=0.05   Surface: Temperature [°C]   Streamline: Velocity field

Max: 30.0

Min: 10.0

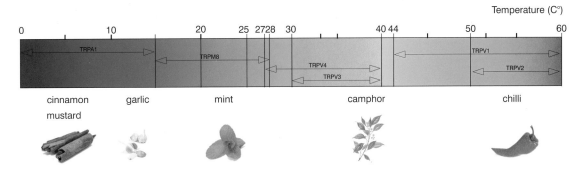

Temperature (C°)

0   10   20   25 2728 30   40 44   50   60

TRPA1

TRPM8

TRPV4

TRPV3

TRPV1

TRPV2

cinnamon   garlic   mint   camphor   chilli
mustard

TRPA1 : transient receptor potential ankrin transmembrane protein 1
TRPM8 : transient receptor potential melastatine 8
TRPV4 : transient receptor potential vanilloïde 4
TRPV3 : transient receptor potential vanilloïde 3
TRPV2 : transient receptor potential vanilloïde 2
TRPV1 : transient receptor potential vanilloïde 1

that has been used, while it will be cold around your feet. So we are starting up a thermodynamic motion around which the house is built. We are introducing two temperatures of 16 and 22 degrees, corresponding to the Swiss recommendations for bedrooms and bathrooms respectively, where you are either lying under the covers or walking around naked. If you lowered the temperature in the bedroom from 'Switzerland' to 'Norway', from 20 to 16 degrees, you would save enormous amounts of energy. The temperature difference sets the air in motion like a kind of miniature Gulf Stream, and creates an invisible landscape of heat. In some places in the house you will have a summer situation, in other places winter. The conditions encourage different functions. Places with 18 degrees will be well suited to kitchen functions for example, while areas with 20 degrees are suitable for living rooms.

You could say that one could almost colonize this landscape as required, or in accordance with the body's sensory preferences?
Precisely – you have a free choice, just like in Switzerland when you go up into the mountains when it gets too warm, or choose to enjoy the warmth in the valleys – you have freedom of movement. We are studying this landscape by working with thermal simulation in computer models, and with the models we can also manipulate its features. Alongside the simulation we are also beginning to develop a spatial geometry that further modulates the thermal landscape in the house. My work is about understanding the issues of climate and atmosphere as tools for architecture, and trying to understand how they can influence the form, programme and function of architecture.

Time to change paradigm: The ecological challenge to architecture

By Wilfried Wang

If it is true that civilization has from early times till today striven for ever greater autonomy from the vicissitudes of time, weather, topography, resources, indeed even fellow beings, then the effort to create a truly sustainable architecture will require Titanian resolve in intellectual perspicacity, behavioural change, as well as hard labour[1].

Architecture's impressive achievements across time shows that the discipline has assisted civilization's strive for this autonomy: we can now live and work anywhere, we can pursue any activity at any time of day and during any season, from inhospitable deserts and polar regions to crowded conurbations. François Dallegret and Reyner Banham's image of the high-energy driven space bubble of 1965 – a form of "well-tempered environment"[2] – has become the idealized icon of civilization's seeming hegemony over the environment, only, we are beginning to realize that the environment is slowly getting even with the dominant form of civilization.

In their bubble, the two protagonists lead a blissfully ignorant, womb-like existence, despite the hard rock and the surrounding climate. At the heart of the bubble is a dense, collapsible piece of survival technology, complete on its own, without any connection to the exterior, without any power supply: autonomy pure and simple.

However, anyone pretending that we can resolve our current difficulties once again by turning our backs to the environment, by sealing ourselves off from the outside, by applying supposedly self-sufficient technological means is not only misleading him or herself, but also anyone else who cares to listen to such a message. Just as individuals used to consuming too much food and thus suffering from obesity can shorten their gastro-intestinal tract or alter the gene that controls weight-gain in order to overcome the problem. These technological interventions will not change their behaviour, on the contrary, they will encourage the persistence of the wery behaviour that led to the obesity in the first place. Over-consumption of food will not necessarily be normalized by such technological interventions. More generally, and this may sound trite and intellectually crude: over-consumption of resources will not be reduced by technological interventions on its own. Technological innovations and interventions, unless carefully integrated into an overall set of cultural principles, will permit the

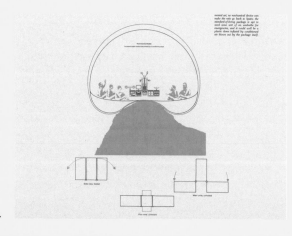

François Dallegret
& Reyner Banham:
*A Home Is Not a
House*, 1965

continuation of the current unsustainable western lifestyle[3].

The clear and painful realization from civilization's process of autonomization in all spheres of life is that we have to understand the all-embracing nature of change that we as a civilization have to undergo in order to avert the extremes of climate change. The pain will lie in the process of adjustment from the influential western lifestyle to specific regional lifestyles. No doubt there will be pain in changing from the current exploitative paradigm that still sees man at the middle of the environment to a paradigm in which homo sapiens is just one species amongst many with equal rights.

By all-embracing I mean cultural: beginning with the cultivation of the local region, the immediate surroundings with sustainable agriculture,

saying good-bye to pharmacologically driven agri-industry, and culminating in the gradual adaptation of nearby resources, which includes pre-existing buildings, to form a stable, yet flexible and adaptable habitat.

We need to confront how deeply the roots of our habits are embedded in time and how this depth of time has made any adjustment in the pattern of behaviour, in our habits, that much more difficult. These habits have been profoundly shaped by gender-based, social, religious and economic ideologies. They have become engrained in our way of thinking to mould our attitudes towards the exploitation of things: people, animals, resources, the environment. The wider the dissemination of such ideologies, the greater the domain of such habits. In differentiation to the idea of the ecological footprint of a set of habits (more a synchronic measure), the depth of time and the breadth of dissemi-nation define the cultural footprint (more a dia-chronic and geographic measure).

The notion of the cultural footprint can help to explain some of the motivations underlying west-ern lifestyle: the dream of life in a freestanding, single-family house in the countryside. Its origin reaches far back to the anti-urban sentiments of ancient societies, including early Greek and Roman civilizations; finding a high point in the Renaissance with the villas of the Veneto and another with Modernist counterpoints such as the Villa Savoie, the Usonian Houses and the Farnsworth House. Today, glancing across the globe, from Chile to China, from Dubai to Dublin, millions of freestand-ing houses can be found as versions that complete the spectrum of possibilities that was once opened by these classical and modernist icons.

In disseminating such icons, the architectural discourse has followed well-trodden paths over the last five hundred years. Two-dimensional repre-sentations in books, lectures and now the internet, from copperplate engravings, black-and-white slides to four-colour photographs, images of items of architecture have been multiplied and deposited in the eager and absorbing minds of architectural students and professionals alike. These icons act as markers. They become goals that are either to be copied, assimilated or overtaken. The conven-tional architectural discourse has functioned in a competitive manner.

In this sense, there has been a separate and ongoing competition within each building type. At the other extreme of the freestanding, single-fam-ily house stands the skyscraper. Its cultural foot-print is almost as old as that of the house, from the Seven Wonders of the Ancient World[4] to the spires of Gothic cathedrals, there has been an unstoppa-ble strive for the tallest and most memorable structure. Size and iconic value have continued to determine the plausibility of such buildings in the last few decades.

Given the notion of the cultural footprint, its depth and breadth of influence on specific habits also determines their projective cast into the future. On this basis, the breaking of a habit will only succeed if we firstly realize that there are such origins and that they are systemically engrained and if we secondly seek and develop a therapy to overcome the habit, not to speak of the selfevident need for the will to change. Therefore, it is by no means clear that the cataclysmic final stage of the deregulated global finance industry will be mir-rored by a final stage of global building culture. While it may be clear to architects and architec-tural critics that the superficial fixation on the pro-duction of images – pretending to be ever more spectacular, overwhelming or memorable – cannot be maintained ad nauseam, and that this produc-tion of images has been specifically tied to the speculative method of financing such projects, it has not yet dawned on enough publishers of archi-tectural journals that they are feeding a dinosaur that is dying as a result of a constipation from ever more repetitive images.

Thus, if we are to confront one of the first, deeply entrenched habits, namely that of vying for new images, searching for the next new style in architecture, in order to be ahead of the curve, to be "with it", to belong to the avant-garde, to be the next shooting star, to achieve fame and wealth, we have to conclude, that, in order to overcome this mind set, all sorts of "reforms" will be necessary. They begin with the way we understand and per-ceive architecture; that is, as a timebased, three-dimensional phenomenon with haptic sculptural and spatial qualities, not as a static, two-dimen-sional composition that is merely to be viewed from a distance, as a pixelated representation. Such a time-based phenomenon involves the understand-ing of buildings as leading individual lives: from inception to construction, from use to maintenance, from adaptation to recycling.

Understanding architecture more in terms of a building's long-term life, its capacity to be adapted, the manner in which it is part of a changing context, opens up a different way of perceiving architecture, of telling the history of architecture. Rather than the rapid kaleidoscopic passage across the nomenclat-ura of outstanding examples of architecture by dead white males, it will become more important to recount the individual complex stories of the fate of a building, from its inception, gestation, construction, adaptation and demise. Even if such icons as the Villa Savoie, Falling Water or the Farnsworth House were still the subject of architectural historiography, their current status would be as important to tell: the life as an icon that has been sold a number of times, that has been renovated and that no longer is used as a residence for one or two people.

The sobering discussion as to how such Modernist icons are to be preserved raises the same reflective questions for apologists of Modernism as for preservationists in general. If the lifestyle that once gave rise to a building no longer exists, to which future uses can a building under a preservation order be put such that it may survive? Architectural historiography needs to recount the stories of the fabrication of styles; the personal networks behind Modernism, for example; the wide spectrum of Modernist options; the dominant and dominated positions within Modernism; its current ideology as well as the formalist moments.

Architectural historiography needs to shift its paradigm from idolizing the same group of dead white males to the critical exposure of their achievements. It needs to stop idealizing the nature of the profession and reveal the realities of daily practice. It should show the logical deadends of the object fetishism into which students and professionals alike have moved. It should reveal the fact that most buildings have experienced one or another form of adaptation in their lives, from airports to hospitals, from parliamentary buildings to speculative offices, from individual houses to garages.

Architectural historiography combined with a reformed architectural theory would take on the task to provide a holistic perception of the long-term life of the built environment. Life-cycle analysis of buildings, hitherto first and foremost undertaken in quantitative terms, thus needs to be extended to qualitative dimensions: what does a building contribute to the collective environment on the one hand, and on the other, how does a building contribute to the well-being of its users, both in its relative static existence and in its ability to change and adapt to new requirements? Lifecycle analysis of buildings should therefore cover not only aspects of embedded energy, energy consumption while in use and its recyclability, but also to what extent its respective typological and tectonic constitution allow for certain degrees of adaptation and how its character and ambience are achieved, and how these qualities contribute to a building's cultural status.

Architectural theory, of which the recent Anglo-Saxon production has paralleled the irresponsible, speculative activities in the deregulated financial industry, needs at last to deal with the evaluation of design quality, how this design quality contributes or hinders the fulfilment of everyday life of societies. We finally need a transparent and comprehensible method of analyzing individual buildings as well as entire complexes. For this, a descriptive method that is able to identify the components of buildings and their overall composition needs to be agreed upon so as to permit the analysis of specific qualities of a building as well as its overall effect in relation to is users. If the profession is unable to achieve this, then the qualitative aspect of a building will always be relegated to the "artistic" domain; the dominant technocrats will continue to control the direction of the broad discourse in the building industry and design quality, the way most architects like to understand it, will remain beyond the bounds of rational dispute. The failure to develop a comprehensible method for the analysis of design quality will thus weaken the architectural profession even further.

However, the current pragmatic approach to architectural design evaluation, seen in the case of design review boards, is an important beginning. All the same, more often than not, panelists base this approach on gut-reactions; the common lack of communicative skills undermining the authority of such review boards. Whether for sensitive contexts such as UNESCO World Heritage Sites or for regional conservation zones, design review boards have established an important instrument for the guaranteeing of appropriate design quality.

These boards should be extended to every building activity in order to select the best possible design solution for any given task. Better to design and review over and over again than to build badly once.

For it is a bitter truth that of one hundred buildings realized only a very small number of these are of the appropriate level of design quality, a fact that relegates the rest to the realm of neglect and therefore premature demolition. Buildings that are not appreciated and indeed loved by their owners, users and the general public are more prone to being knocked down at the earliest opportunity than those that are appreciated and respected. The clearest evidence of such a practice can be seen in the case of many post-Second World War buildings.

Architectural theory therefore needs to develop communicative methods by which design qualities can be identified, evaluated and discussed in public and with the public. We need to sensitize ourselves and the public to qualities in architecture that may lie buried or are simply overlooked. The purpose of such identification and sensitization is to demystify architectural design on the one hand – to avoid the public being misled by the attachment of words to buildings or their components such as "this skyscraper will be 1776 feet tall" to commemorate the year of the declaration of independence of the USA as if this were visible or significant – and on the other hand to cultivate real sensibilities that ultimately lead to a greater and wider sense of interest in and ownership of, respect and care for a building.

Without a generally accessible method of evaluating building designs, the building industry will quite understandably focus on the quantifiable, objectifiable, rationally describable aspects of an architectural design. In this way, the resource flows, emissions, toxins, costs, etc. will be measurable and will form the exclusive means of assessment. This will lead to the renewed overemphasis of the non-haptic, non-sensual, economic-rationalist dimension of construction. The last time that a renewal in building culture was attempted in a wholesale mode was a century ago. It was then that the social aim of providing high-design standards for everyday needs in the service of a broad public was pursued, only to end in disaster, as countless analysts and critics have noted in the past decades.

The dialectic of this first enlightenment was most succinctly recounted by Max Horkheimer and Theodor W. Adorno in the last years of the Second World War[5], later followed in the field of urban design by Alexander Mitscherlich[6]. Parallel to the betrayal of the first enlightenment's goals of freeing mankind from the ills of religious mythology, superstitious ignorance and feudal tyranny only to find these supplanted by the tyranny of rationalism, the enlightenment promise in the built environment was betrayed by architects who denied the raison d'etre of the aesthetic dimension to building culture. In focussing on the rational side of such production, the dominant economic-rationalist, technocratic actors in the building industry successfully ignored entire fields of human needs. The cohesion of the urban fabric, albeit insanitary in its speculative density at the end of the 19th century, was supplanted with mono-functional, freestanding and thereby isolating residential slabs in the post-Second World War years. Everything was sanitized, ethnic cleansing the ultima ratio.

If there is a choice, then the second enlightenment must set an end to the selective understanding of habitats of species, including that of homo sapiens. It can no longer be "to each his own", but must build on John Dunne's dictum "no man is an island" to expand to "no species is an island", that all are involved in this world; it must transcend Charles Darwin's insight of the survival of the fittest to the survival of the whole. For if civilization does not have the intelligence to deduce from the current state of the globe that it is homo sapiens that needs to adapt in such a way as to give more space to other species, not to continue with the removal of the basis of other species' eco-systems, but to fundamentally challenge our habits, to change the second enlightenment must broaden the basis of understanding of our world beyond the quantifiable to include the qualifiable. If sustainability as a principle is to be established as a measure for a new paradigm, the associated lifestyle must be defined in quantitative and qualitative terms as global goals and standards. The second enlightenment must acknowledge the rights of disadvantaged groups around the globe and enable them reach the global goals and standards, while the advantaged groups must be prepared to renounce their title to resources that would otherwise prevent the disadvantaged groups to achieve the globally acknowledged goals. Without such a rebalancing of the use of resources, all talk of sustainability and controlling climate change will remain just that.

Western societies have long ago plundered their forests, land, lakes and seas. They have no right to demand that other, less developed nations stop plundering their forests, land, lakes and seas now. Western societies have polluted the air, caused acid rain, sprayed DDT, produced dioxin for PVC, invented emissions trading, are attempting to control the agri-industry by selling one-timeonly seeds. Their moral status in the eyes of non-western societies is essentially non-existent.

Western architecture, that suggests that emissions can be controlled by producing ever more spectacular, ever more novel, technologically jam-packed free-standing, new buildings, indeed entire cities, are equally lacking in credibility if they do not show that these new buildings and cities consume less resources and emit less green house gases in their gestation, use and recycling phases than that which stood in their place before, not to speak of the difference in aesthetic quality.

If there is to be a second modern movement in architecture based on this change in paradigm and informed by the second enlightenment, then a building will come into existence when there is a real demand for it, it will be carefully designed and thoroughly evaluated, it will be built slowly, it will cost a lot, it will require intensive craftsmanship, it will seek to have a long physical as well as aesthetic life expectancy, it will use all sorts of material brought together from around the project site, it will supercede any notion of "innovation", it will appear to be a minor growth within a vast sea of pre-existing structures, it will quietly integrate itself with its context and will integrate all components essential to its survival, including the necessary technology, it will look – if at all distinctive – heterogeneous. Any entirely new building will consume fewer resources in its construction, use and recycled stage; will emit fewer green house gases and, most importantly, will be of a higher design quality than the object it replaces.

Most surprisingly, a building of the second modern movement will be comprehensible, will be made of the materials that represent it, will create an atmosphere that will stand prolonged contemplation and will thus engender more sensations than most icons of the first modern movement, including a sense of participation, of ownership, of respect and of care. Sensations that alone guarantee the building's sustained existence.

1. See an extended presentation of this thesis by the author, Introductory Essay, in: *World Architecture: A critical Mosaic 1900-2000, vol. 3*, gen. ed. Kenneth Frampton, vol. ed. Wilfried Wang & Helga Kusolitsch, Vienna/New York, Springer, 2000, p. XVII-XXIX.
2. Reyner Banham, *A Home is not a House*, with ill. by François Dallegret, Art in America, No. 2, New York, April 1965.
3. By this term is meant the life-style framed by male, white, Christian, Anglo-Saxon capitalism.
4. The Pyramid of Giza, the Colossus of Rhodes, the Tomb of King Mausolos at Halicarnassus, and the Lighthouse of Alexandria.
5. Max Horkheimer & Theodor W. Adorno, *The Dialectic of the Enlightenment*, originally published in German *Dialektik der Aufklärung. Philosophische Fragmente*, Amsterdam, Querido, 1947.
6. Alexander Mitscherlich, *Die Unwirtlichkeit unserer Städte, Thesen zur Stadt der Zukunft*, Frankfurt am Main, Suhrkamp, 1965.

Wilfried Wang is the O'Neil Ford Centennial Professor in Architecture at the University of Texas at Austin and founder of the Berlin practice of Hoidn Wang Partner. He studied architecture in London, co-edited 9H magazine and co-directed the 9H Gallery, and directed the German Architecture Museum (1995-2000). Wang is the author of various monographs and topographs on the architecture of the 20th-century. He chairs the Erich-Schelling Foundation and the design review board of the UNESCO World Heritage Site of Wismar, is a member of the design review board of Munich Airport, a member of CICA, an honorary member of the Federation of German Architects (BDA) and of the Royal Swedish Academy of Fine Arts.

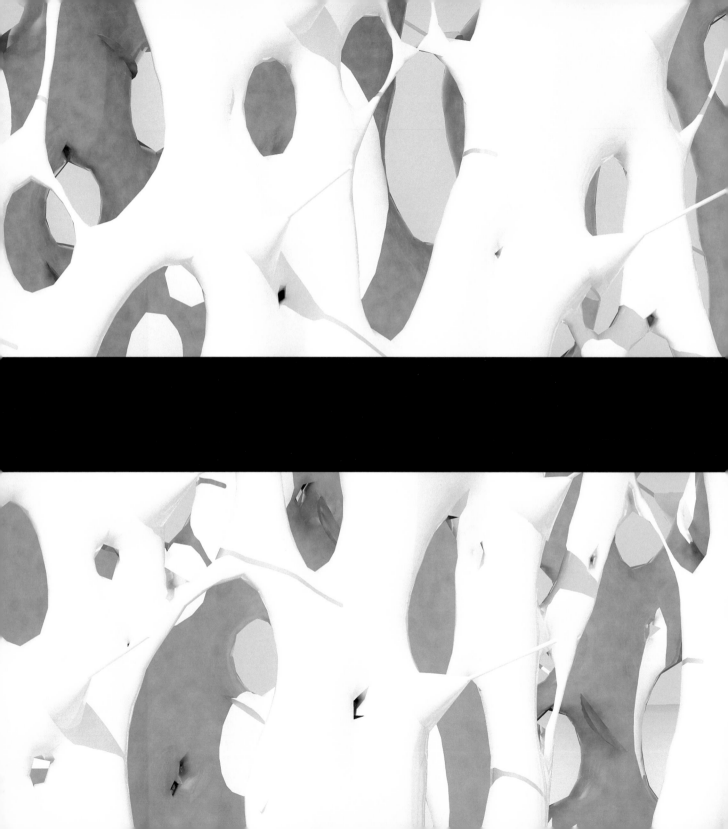

METABOLISM

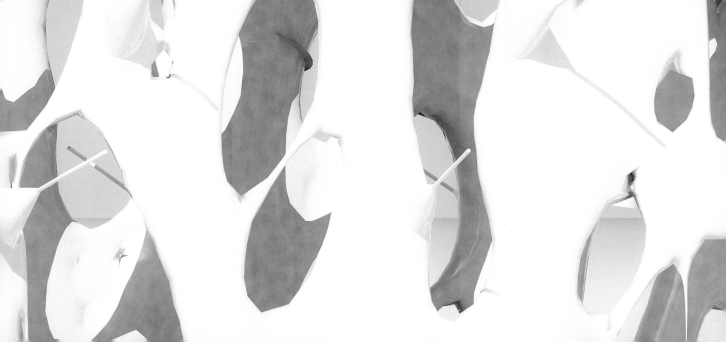

Cradle 2 Cradle

We must design evolution

The buildings of the future will regularly replace elements just as we humans replace our cells in the course of life – this sets up a new framework for the substance, lifetime and recycling of materials. Cradle to Cradle is the name of a philosophy which, with inspiration from nature's ecosystems, rethinks the way we make our products and buildings. Instead of conceiving our products from cradle to grave – from raw material to waste – we must conceive the whole lifetime of the product as a cycle where nothing goes to waste and the things we use can even contribute surplus to the production system. This design strategy is currently being developed and used in consumer products, whole buildings and working routines by major companies like Ford and Nike.

"If humans are truly going to prosper, we will have to learn to imitate nature's high effective cradle to cradle system of nutrient flow and metabolism, in which the very concept of waste does not exist"...

(McDonough & Braungart, 2002)

The lessons of nature

Cradle to Cradle Design's strategy of eco-effectiveness is rooted in the systems of the natural world, which are not efficient at all, but effective. Consider the cherry tree. Each spring it brings forth thousands of blossoms, which then fall in piles to the ground – not very efficient. But the fallen blossoms become food for other living things. The tree's abundance of blossoms is both safe and useful, contributing to the health of a thriving, interdependent system. And the tree spreads multiple positive effects – making oxygen, transpiring water, creating habitat, and more.

Eco-effectiveness seeks to design industrial systems that emulate the healthy abundance of nature. The central design principle of eco-effectiveness is 'waste equals food'.

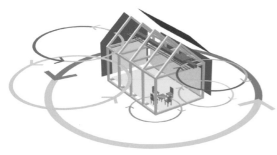

STUFF
1 day - 1 month

SKIN
20 years

SETTING
3-30 years

STRUCTURE
30-300 years

SYSTEMS
7-15 years

SITE
eternal

Imagine your house as a tree and the city as a forest

Tower of Tomorrow is a skyscraper that works like a tree, makes oxygen, distills water, produces energy, and changes with the seasons. The shape of the building is aerodynamic, reducing the impact of the wind, while its curved form reduces the amount of material needed for construction, increases structural stability and maximizes enclosed space. Flora abounds, with a green roof and three-storey atrium gardens planned on the western side of the building. As for water, the waste water from sinks and bathtubs would be recycled and used for irrigation in the building's gardens; and the waste water from gardens could further be re-used in toilets. The southern façade would be made of about 100,000 square feet of photovoltaic panels that convert sunlight into electricity. The robust system could provide up to 40 per cent of the building's needs. A combined heat-and-power plant would also be installed, to be fueled by natural gas, which could supply the power that the solar panels cannot.

All products, from building materials to furnishings, could be recycled or returned safely to the earth.

The biological and technical nutrient cycles

How can a building become part of nature's cycle for re-use and nutrient exchanges? How can our modern technological consumer goods do the same? Instead of the symbol for recycling that we know so well, we should in future represent our recycling by two different circles.

Products can be composed either of materials that biodegrade and become food for biological cycles, or of technical materials that stay in closed-loop technical cycles, in which they continually circulate as valuable nutrients for industry. In order for these two metabolisms to remain healthy, valuable, and successful, great care must be taken to avoid contaminating one with the other (C2C, P. 104).

The Mirra Chair

The Mirra Chair is an example of a product that can be re-used in accordance with Cradle to Cradle's two nutrient cycles. When the chair was designed it contained 40 different materials constituted by 200 different chemicals.
In collaboration with Cradle to Cradle Design Chemistry, MBDC, the manufacturer, Herman Miller, evaluated the ease of disassembling products on the basis of four questions:
1. Can the component be separated out as a homogeneous material, with no other materials attached? Mixed materials, if inseparable, have little or no value in recycling programmes. The goal is for disassembly to create individual components that may have value when recycled.
2. Can the component be disassembled using common tools – a screwdriver, a hammer and a pair of pliers? The goal is for the chairs to be easily disassembled anywhere in the world.
3. Does it take less than 30 seconds for one person to disassemble the component? The product development team disassembled many products and concluded that 30 seconds is too long for the removal of any component.
4. Is the material identifiable and marked? If parts are not marked, then disassemblers will not know which recycling bin to place them in.

The result is a chair that the consumer can dismantle into all its components, such that worn parts can be replaced over time and put back into either a biodegradable recycling process or a technical recycling process.

Form follows evolution

To eliminate the concept of waste means to design things – products, packaging, and systems – from the very beginning on the understanding that waste does not exist. It means that the valuable nutrients contained in the materials shape and determine the design:

"Form follows evolution, not just function".
(McDonough & Braungart, 2002)

Nike considered

Nike is an example of a company that is working to introduce Cradle to Cradle at all levels. Both individual types of shoes and the factory building are created on the basis of Cradle to Cradle design strategies.

In 1996 Nike contracted William McDonough + Partners to design a new, state-of-the-art campus for its European headquarters in The Netherlands. A complex of five new buildings, the campus was designed to integrate the indoors with the surrounding environment, tapping into local energy flows to create healthy, beneficial relationships between nature and human culture.

The buildings are organized around a central green and form four smaller courtyards around the perimeter, each landscaped with native plants. The orientation of the buildings and the window design maximize daylight while minimizing heat gain. Ground-source heat pumps use the constant temperature of the earth for heating and cooling. On the roofs, cisterns collect 3.9 million litres of storm water annually for landscape irrigation and other greywater uses.

The overall goal for Nike was to eliminate the concept of waste in product design, using materials, energy and resources that can be readily recycled, renewed or reabsorbed back into nature; to eliminate all substances that are known or suspected to be harmful to human health and the natural system. An additional intention was to develop financial structures that promote greater product stewardship in design, engineering, and manufacturing, as well as to create new financial models to reflect the full cost of doing business. The management of materials presents some of the same logistical challenges that Nike is facing in its management of labour practices in the factories of its suppliers. These efforts can go hand in hand. As Nike implements its palette of positively defined, healthful materials, it creates healthier workplaces and communities.

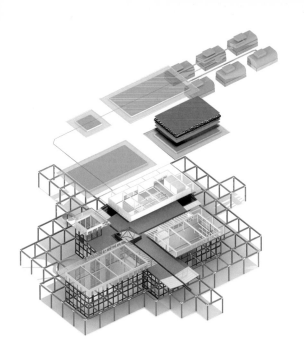

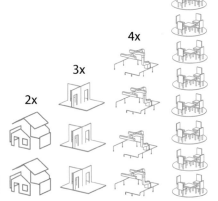

MATERIAL RECOVERY

Number of times materials and systems
cycle through a building in a single lifetime

8x — 7th generation

4x

3x

2x

1x — 1th generation

| site | structure | skin | setting | systems | stuff |

The lifetime of Buildings
The buildings of the future will regularly replace
elements just as we humans replace our cells in
the course of life – this sets up a new framework
for the substance, lifetime and recycling of materials. In future, houses will become separable so
that step by step they can be transformed in
keeping with the needs of coming generations.

United Bottle Project

2007
Instant Architects, Dirk Hebel, Tobias Klauser,
Hanspeter Logo, Jörg Stollmann

The intersection of local and global circuits forms the basis of the project "United Bottle." The "United Bottle" scenario is based on the idea that newly designed PET bottles can be taken out of the regular recycling circuits in the event of crisis or specific demand to be used as instant building materials for temporary housing. During a state of emergency, relief organizations and NGOs face two major challenges: the distribution of drinking water and the construction of emergency shelters.

"United Bottle" is both a PET water bottle and a prefabricated building unit. Leading producers of mineral water as well as NGOs use it for their water sales or distribution.

The bottles are integrated into the regular PET recycling circuits. They arrive in foil-wrapped six-packs on pallets at the local stores and are collected and recycled with the aid of a bottle deposit system. In the event of crisis, the bottles are taken out of these circuits and distributed via the UNHCR (United Nations High Commissioner for Refugees) into the relevant zones. In combination with a mechanical water pump, they are used for local water distribution. "United Bottle" allows for solar drinking-water disinfection (SODIS). For local distribution purposes, nine bottles form a stable unit that can be carried by a single person. The tuck-in system generates secure connections that resist torsion. This system also enhances the suitability of the bottle as a construction material. In combination with UN tent blankets, for example, "United Bottle" functions as a solid shelter construction unit and as a water reservoir. Filled with local materials, "United Bottle" turns into a construction material for temporary or even long-term shelters. Local knowledge of building techniques, improvisation, and consumer waste are used to build small free-standing buildings and to extend and repair existing structures.

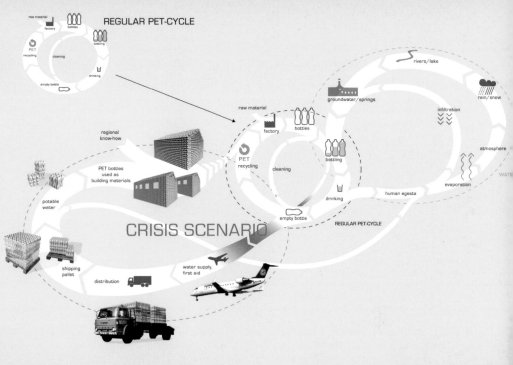

REGULAR PET-CYCLE

CRISIS SCENARIO

REGULAR PET-CYCLE

Olzweg

Paris, 2006
Architect: R&Sie(n)... Paris
Creative team: François Roche, Stephanie Lavaux,
Jean Navarro,
With partners:
Pierre Huyghe, artist
Mathieu Lehanneur, furniture designer
Stephan Henrich, robotics designer
Nicholas Green, facade engineer
Sibat, basic engineer
Julien Blervaque, script programmer &
Alexander Römer, Agnes Vidal, Daniel Fernán-dez Florez
Key dimensions: 5000 m²
Client: FRAC Orléans / Région Centre
Location: Orléans
Cost: € 5m
Design of a museum of experimental architec-ture (FRAC)

Scenario

1. In the courtyard of the FRAC an aggregate of glass sticks generates a 'smearing' of the exist-ing building as a 'Body Without Organs' (an unachieved process of construction) with a laby-rinth of glass
2. Construction and cleaning procedures are robot-assisted to introduce randomization and uncertainty in the final form. The labyrinth can be reprogrammed during construction itself
3. The elements of glass come from a public glass-recycling process. This reduces the raw material costs and involves the inhabitants of the agglomeration in the "work to be done" story
4. The construction schedule is planned to extend over more than 10 years
5. The use of individual RIFD-PDAs induces visi-tors to lose themselves willingly in the glass maze and redefine their XYZ positions according to the specificities of an exhibition (PDA with sound, video and local GPS).

A robot builds with the irregularity and wildness of nature: a continuous process that has no ulti-mate goal. A 'Body without Organs' refers to the virtual element of mankind, the part that can potentially follow other paths, and reflexes, than those by which the physical body is controlled. The construction depends on the inhabitants' consumption of wine and recycled bottles.

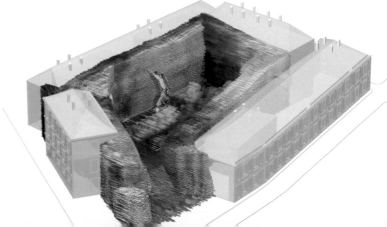

Paper Log Houses

Shigeru Ban, Tokyo/New York/Paris

Temporary "log" houses built for the victims of the earthquakes in Kobe, Kaynasli and Bhuj.

Shigeru Ban's more fundamental interest and passion is the development of the paper tube as the main building structure. The case study houses called the PTS Series are examples of paper tube constructions. These are a series of experimental houses based on the idea of using standardized non-architectural products – that is, paper tubes – in an entirely different context. As well as creating more free space, the PTS technology establishes a completely new concept where building materials are entirely recycled after the building purposes have been served. Paper tubes are readily available in various thicknesses and diameters. These are the two factors that determine the weight they can support. Recycled cardboard can be moulded into load-bearing columns, bent into beautiful trusses and quickly assembled; it can also be made waterproof and fire-resistant.

Kobe, Japan, 1994
The foundations consist of donated beer crates loaded with sandbags. The walls are made from paper tubes 4 mm thick and 106 mm in diameter, with tenting material for the roof. The 1.8 m space between houses was used as a common area. For insulation, a waterproof sponge tape backed with adhesive is sandwiched between the paper tubes of the walls. The cost of materials for one 52 square metre unit is below $2000. The units are easy to dismantle, and the materials easily disposed of or recycled.

Kaynasli, Turkey, 2000
On the basis of the experience from the shelter in Kobe, Japan, some improvements were made to adapt the units to the environment in Turkey. For example one unit was 3 x 6 m, a different, slightly larger configuration due to the standard plywood size in Turkey as well as the country's larger average family size. Secondly, there was more insulation. Shredded waste paper was inserted inside the tubes along the walls and fibre-glass in

the ceiling, while cardboard and plastic sheets were used for more insulation, depending on the needs of the resident.

Bhuj, India, 2001

What makes the Indian log house unique is the foundations and the roof. Rubble from destroyed buildings was used for the foundations instead of beer crates, which could not be found in this area. This was covered with a traditional mud floor. In the roof, split bamboo was used for the rib vaults and whole bamboo for the ridge beams. A locally woven cane mat was placed over the bamboo ribs, followed by a clear plastic tarpaulin as protection against rain, then another cane mat. Ventilation was provided through the gables, where small holes in the mats allowed air to circulate. This ventilation also allowed cooking to be done inside, with the added benefit of repelling mosquitoes.

S-House

Böheimkirchen, 2005
GrAT – Centre for Appropiate Technology,
Vienna

In the S-House no metallic components or synthetic materials were used in the entire building. Only wood was used for the static construction. The facade was built as a structure made of wooden boards and straw bales pressed and mounted without thermal bridging. This straw proofing was provided with a layer of clay plaster and a wooden casing. Windproofing is ensured by the wooden board construction. The south facade is fully glazed and the entire building is 'packaged' with straw, providing optimum heat insulation. The heat is captured by the large surface-glazed south facade and distributed over a mechanical ventilation and exhaust system into the building. The air is transported by specially developed wooden channels into all areas of the building. In the ground floor, a stone floor acts as heat retainer. These stone tiles are the only mineral material that is used in the S-HOUSE. An earth commutator takes care of temperature balancing: during winter it prevents glacial formation in the ventilation system and during sum-

mer it serves as a cooling device. The building stands on a sub-ventilated building slab, which is supported by individual footings. This facilitated a significant reduction in the use of mineral resources compared with a conventional foundation; in addition, this construction does not allow accumulation of cold and humid air in the floor slab area. This optimizes the degree of insulation in the floor construction. The roof has been designed as a membranous roof, made of a 'flying' wooden construction mounted over the straw-insulated wooden ceiling, covered with a rubber membrane and 'greened'.

The use of raw materials (clay and straw) available on-site or in the region minimizes environmental pollution caused by the manufacture and transportation of building materials.

Stock Orchard Street 9-10

London, 2001
Sarah Wigglesworth, London

9 Stock Orchard Street is the architect's own house and associated studio office in Islington, North London. The building uses natural and recyclable materials and a number of innovative technologies based around principles of sustainable design, many of which are being used in an urban context for the first time.

The design uses passive energy principles, with the heavily insulated straw bale wall wrapping around the north-east and north-west elevations, whilst the south elevation is glazed to capture heat from the sun. The tower acts as a thermal flue, catching the wind and encouraging natural ventilation to cool the house in the summer. Materials have been chosen with a view to limiting their environmental impact. The north wall is made of standard straw bales, stacked between loadbearing timber ladders and protected on the outside with a rainscreen. The living areas are open plan, designed to accommodate flexible living patterns, whilst the bedroom wing is conceived of as a warm haven, wrapped by a protective wall of straw.

Other innovative materials include cement bags, for acoustic protection against the railway line, a duvet type cladding to the office and the use of gabion walls filled with recycled concrete. Rainwater is collected to irrigate the roof meadow and feed toilets and washing machines. Further water savings are made through the incorporation of one of the first composting toilets to be used in the UK in an urban situation.

Finally, it is in the nature of the project that it will never be 'finished'; the building is designed to evolve over time – the cement bags will decay, the library will steadily grow upwards to occupy the tower, the roof will get shaggy, colours will fade. As it is lived in, amendments are being made to improve the building and extend the brief by adding new elements (garden shed, light shelf).

Learning from Nature

The 3XN Pavilion at the Louisiana

Building sustainably is not least a matter of learning from nature. 3XN works to create architecture that forms behaviour. One of the most important aspects of sustainable behaviour is to live in harmony with nature's own 'housekeeping', of which mankind forms a part. And one of the most important aspects of architectural behaviour is therefore to make nature's own systems a part of our culture. The natural systems are based on great and small cyclical movements, from the light years of the heavenly bodies to the diurnal rhythms of living organisms. Human beings and their houses are part of nature's cycle, and the architecture of the future will be the architecture that is able to learn from nature's methods of managing energy, climate, landscape and materials.

In form, function, execution and life cycle, 3XN's Pavilion is an example of design based on biomimicry (from Greek *bios*, life, and *mimesis*, imitation). By imitating and being inspired by natural systems, we can develop processes and methods of design and architecture that will help to meet the basic human need for a roof over one's head in a sustainable way.

The Pavilion takes the form of a Moebius Strip; its endlessness expresses the continuity and eternal cycles of nature. Architecture often seems like a rupture in nature and the totality of the landscape, but that is pure convention. In the future architecture will to a much greater extent be created in harmony with its surroundings; the better we get at understanding and imitating the systems of nature, the more holistic architecture can become, and the closer will be the bond between nature and human construction.

The Pavilion meets three basic human needs: the need for shelter, for rest and for contact. The strip is both roof and bench – at the same time an experience of nature and space. It enters into a cycle that uses a minimum of new materials in a recyclable and fully biodegradable physical framework. It purifies the air like a tree by using

Visitor Dynamics

A dynamic interchange of energy between the visitors and the pavilion is obtained by the kinetic energy generated by the feet of thousands of visitors walking on the floor of the pavillion. The energy collected is transfered to the integrated lighting system wich will make an immediate response tothe visitors interaction.

Material Dynamics

The materials are written into a clear narrative of recycling into a technocircle: All the materials of the actual structure are obtained from recycling, upgradir the material of this architectural sculpture, and will be further upgraded upon destruction into base material that can be used in new production lines.

Pavillion Dynamics

The behavior of the material used in the pavillion allows for a dynamic interaction with its surrounding. Just like a tree purifies the air, the pavillion has the same function converting industrial smog into clean air. The use of phase-changing materials results in an exchange of energy during the daily shifts in temperature.

the energy of the sun to break down pollutants. It produces its own energy in collaboration with the visitor.

It consists of bio-composites, which have the same properties as plastic composites, fibreglass and polyester, but are fully biodegradable into the elements of which they consist. It accumulates its own energy for lighting by means of solar energy and the kinetic energy that arises when the visitors walk around on the strip. It demonstrates the ability of phase-changing materials to act as heat absorbers and heat emitters when the temperature and weather change. Its thermochromatic surface treatment shows the tracks left by the visitors when they touch the ribbon. At the end of its life it can be broken down and can enter into the biological metabolism of nature.

A joint collaboration

The Louisiana Museum of Modern Art invited the Danish architecture firm 3XN to design a pavillion demonstrating cutting edge possibilities within sustainable and intelligent materials.

The result is a pavillion that is build of bio composites with integrated intelligens that creates a dynamic interaction with its physical surroundings and its users. The Sustainable Pavillion could never have been realized without the tremendous effort, expertise and joint collaboration with all of the below mentioned:

Project partners
3XN
architects and project manegement
COWI
engineering and light design
Stage One Freeform Composites
production and installation
BASF, the chemical company
phase changing materials
Micronal PCM, cimate control
phase changing materials
Ashland Inc.
producer of bioresin
TransFurans Chemicals
producer of bioresin
Amorim Cork Composites
producer of cork
Libeco-Lagae
producer of natural fibers
ENKEV Natural Fibres
producer of natural fibers
Flex Cell
producer of flexible photo voltaic
Phillips
producer of led light
Scenetek
intallation of eletrical components
Noliac Motion
producer of piezoelectric materials
Optima Projects Limited
composite counseling
NetComposites Ldt
network within composites
Danish Technological Institute
selfcleaning counseling
Risø National Laboratory DTU
composite testing

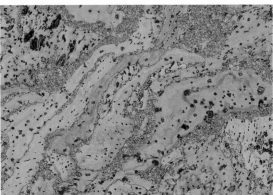

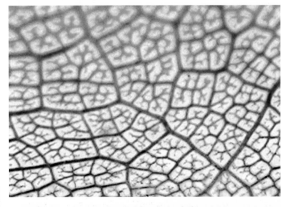

Self cleaning

Phase changing

Piezo electric

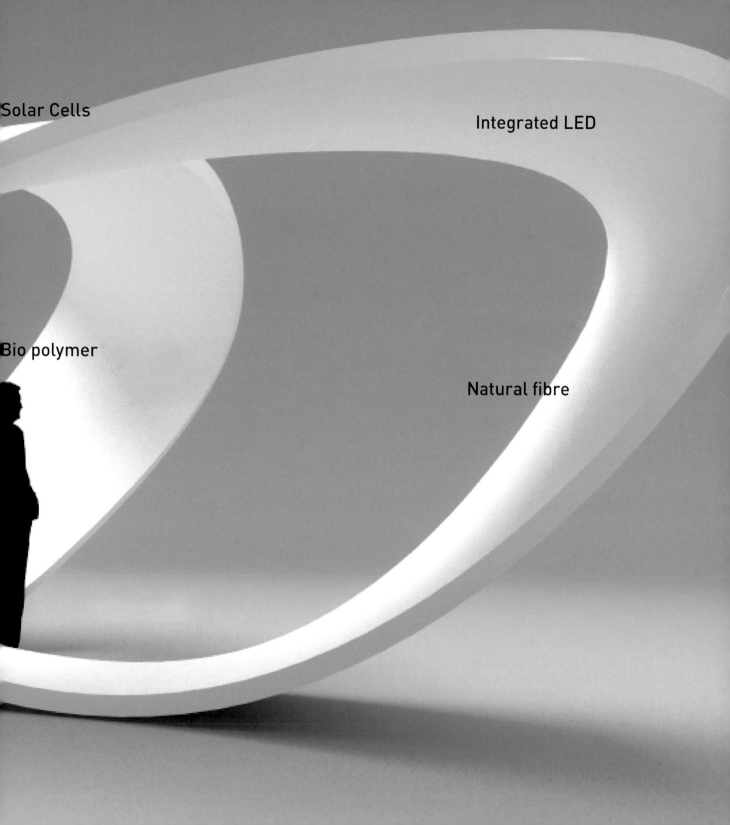

Solar Cells

Integrated LED

Bio polymer

Natural fibre

The Material Future

By Kasper Guldager Jørgensen

The ages of civilization have typically been named after the materials we have used: stone, bronze, iron. Today the silicon of the computer might be a candidate for such a nominator, but the world is no longer dominated by just one material; there are many different, very important materials, and the combinations they permit are particularly interesting.

New materials are very much a matter of new scientific knowledge. The volume of research in the world of biology, physics and chemistry doubles every ten months – a rate of development that remarkably parallels that of the development of computing power.

In architecture the word design is mainly associated with the design of buildings and objects – that is, external objects that relate to the human scale. In the world of materials, design is something internal. The development of production methods on the micro scale has led to far greater control of how we design and construct new materials. This kind of design is mainly invisible to the eye.

The materials of the future are already a reality. They exist in many of the products we use in our everyday life, and they can help us to find answers to many of the challenges we face in the development of sustainable architecture. The question is not which material you want to choose, but which properties are desirable for the specific job. Ultimately, the periodic table of elements defines our building-blocks.

The following two sections describe two of the most fascinating material groups; the intelligent or 'smart' materials and the materials of nanotechnology.

Intelligent materials

The intelligent materials are also called responsive materials, because they react to external stimuli such as changes in temperature, pressure, movement, electricity, radiation and the action of chemicals. This means they can change form, structure, colour or generate energy in accordance with the conditions around them, which opens up a brand new understanding of materials where they can interact directly with the architecture and the users.

Conventional materials are *static*. Usually their function is to withstand external influences such as pressure, tension and temperature effects. Smart (or intelligent) materials are *dynamic,* since they *react* to external influences. This is a fundamental difference that inspires new thinking about the use of materials. Instead of building passive constructions and climate screens as hitherto, we can use intelligent materials for dynamic buildings, where functions and information can in principle be installed anywhere; intelligent systems with the scope to adapt to the users. Houses that react to changes in temperature and light, or constructions that can reinforce themselves at peak loads, for example during storms and earthquakes.

Intelligent materials already exist to a great extent in our everyday life. Many products contain monitoring or responsive functions – for examples windows that tone down harsh sunlight, surfaces that change colour at different temperatures, or windows that are temperature-sensitive and open and close automatically.

At the overall level there are two categories of intelligent materials: property-changing materials and energy-exchanging materials. Let us look a little closer at the two groups.

Property-changing materials

Intelligent materials that change in response to a changed context – chemical, mechanical, optical, electrical, magnetic, or changes in temperature – are called property-changing materials. They can be divided into a number of sub-groups, including:

Chromatic materials, which are a group of smart materials that inevitably fascinate any designer because of their ability to change their optical properties and thus change colour. They are used to indicate changes in light, heat, pressure, acidity and electricity. For example a thermochromatic coffee cup changes colour when it is filled with hot coffee, and an electrochromatic window can be dimmed by running a current through it.

Phase-changing materials, which are able to store and release large quantities of energy. They change between solid and liquid form with shifts in pressure or temperature. These processes are reversible, which means that phase-changing materials can undergo infinitely many phase shifts without degenerating. There are for example microcapsules with phase-changing parafin that can be calibrated to store and release energy at room temperature.

Electroactive materials are either polymers or metallic materials that are woven into textiles, making them electrically conductive. With the increasing use of electronic equipment in our time, current-carrying materials are particularly interesting.

Energy-exchanging materials

Intelligent materials that transform energy from one state to another to start a process or change form are called energy-exchanging materials. They function with the aid of an external control.

Luminescent materials light up when they absorb energy – a phenomenon known for example from natural phosphorescence. Many properties, including the colour of light, can be adjusted for the desired purpose. The use of photoluminescent or electroluminescent materials can make things luminous. We know this from among other things diving lights and organic LED light, which is said to be the light source of the future.

Piezoelectric crystals react by creating an electrical current when they are affected by mechanical forces. This effect is reversible. If an electric current is applied to such crystals they change form. Piezoelectric materials are therefore used as sensors and actuators. In the architectural perspective kinetic energy from wind and humans can be converted into light, mechanical cooling or other energy-requiring functions.

Shape memory materials are either metals or polymers. It is characteristic of both groups that they return to their original form or geometry after a deformation. For example a suture has been developed for surgical operations that ties a knot in itself. If the thread is tied around a blood vessel and actuated by body heat it goes back to its original form.

Nanotechnological materials

Nanotechnology is an interdisciplinary science from which new knowledge of the molecular world arises - a mixture of medical and material research spiced with mechanical and electrical engineering. It is in the area between these different sciences that nanotechnology plays its role.

Since there is no fixed formula for what defines a nanomaterial, it can be difficult to speak of a special category of materials. Nanotechnology is characterized by the use of very small components which by their nature or through manipulation can create new properties which can be added to and improve existing materials. In reality these are materials with no real materiality.

First and foremost the scale is fascinating,

because it is so inconceivably small; a nanometre is a billionth of a metre, a unit one hundred thousandth of the thickness of an average human hair.

The aim of working on the nano scale is that the properties of the materials function quiet differently at the nano level than at the macro level. The world as we know it functions on the macro scale, where cause and effect are predictable and conform strictly to the prevailing physical and chemical laws. On the nano scale things work differently. The sizes of the particles are a critical factor. Quite different conditions apply when the effects of the force of gravity are neutralized, and electrostatic and quantum-mechanical factors take over. This is where the strength of nanotechnology lies. If one can manipulate structures on the nano scale, one can influence the properties on the macro scale, and thus produce brand new materials and processes. Nanotechnology is in the borderland between atoms and molecules, a world where the functional properties of the materials are dictated by the composition of atoms.

Nanotechnology is expected to influence almost all industries – including the construction industry. For many years to come the developments will be visible because of the improved properties of traditional materials like concrete, glass, composites, insulating materials and even wood. Materials will become stronger, lighter, more durable and cheaper. In other words the development of new materials has a very promising future – and this is not just speculative futurology, for there are already many materials that take advantage of nanotechnology.

Functional surfaces

'Thin film' could also be called functional film, since it is a transparent coating with specific properties. Thin film is used everywhere, all the way from ultraviolet filters that protect us from the rays of the sun to teflon surfaces that make the facades of buildings easy to maintain.

The self-cleaning function of the lotus leaf is a good example of the way modern technology can imitate the properties of nature. Using nanotechnology one can recreate the leaf's water-repellent property. On the face of it you might think that a water-repellent surface should be as smooth as possible, but on closer scrutiny you discover that the structures on a lotus leaf are uneven. Today imitating this structure has led to the production of self-

cleaning glass. Experiments are also being done with other alternatives to conventional glass; for example a cellulose-structured thin film is being developed that is completely transparent and biodegradable.

Biochemically active materials

A material that is also much sought-after in the nano world is silver. It keeps its form, it has the same colour in all kinds of weather and on the whole it is a chemically very stable material. But in very small quantities it behaves quite differently. Nano-sized silver particles are extremely reactive and have long been used to clean materials and sterilize surfaces.

The same is true of titanium dioxide, used as what is called a photocatalyst. This is a relatively new material in Europe, but is widely used in Japan. It is activated by the ultraviolet rays of the sun and creates self-cleaning and air-purifying surfaces. Photocatalytic surfaces are used to maintain facades, roofing panels, bridges and roads. Because of their self-cleaning properties they are also used to keep hospitals bacteria-free and to purify the air in offices and restaurants. The use of such surfaces improves the air quality by something between twenty and seventy per cent. In other words it is a material which, used on facades in cities, could solve problems caused by smog and other pollution.

Nanostructured solids

Nanotechnology can also be used to make solid materials. One example is electrospinning, where you weave textiles by means of an electromagnetic field. In electrospun textiles the fibres are only a few atoms thick – in other words the diameter is less than the wavelength of visible light, which makes the fibres invisible to the human eye. They are used in many contexts, from biochemically active materials to soundproofing and air filters.

The 'hottest' nanomaterial today is carbon nanotubes. The special feature of the material is that it is based on the smallest building block in nature – the atom. It has become possible to control the way atoms arrange themselves so they form tubes of carbon atoms with a diameter of one nanometre. This is a good example of how far 'bottom-up' processes have come. Today nanotubes are used as additives to strengthen composites and other structural materials.

In the near future nanotubes can be used to produce the phantom material 'buckypaper'. This is a material where long nanotubes are used to weave textiles that are then stacked or laminated as a composite. It looks like ordinary paper, and is ten times lighter than steel, but up to five hundred times as strong. It has been predicted that this will transform the way we build everything – from highrises to aircraft.

The environment race

For several decades the construction sector has been described as an area where nanotechnology will bring about huge changes. Nevertheless nanomaterials are used to a very limited extent in buildings today. This is due to their high cost and the lack of experience from reference projects.

On the other hand there is nothing that can stimulate development better than a clearly defined task, for example a Moon mission or a Formula One race. The task that is more evident than any other today is that we have to solve the environmental problems facing the world – and the biggest ones are created in the building sector. Technology is only a means to an end; the true challenge is to exploit the potential of re-inventing our use of materials.

Kasper Guldager Jørgensen is an architect and is head of Research and Development for the architectural office 3XN, writes for the Danish Architectural Press and teaches at the School of Architecture of the Royal Danish Academy of Fine Arts.

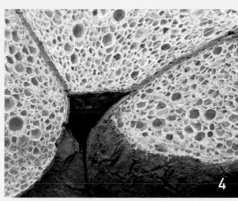

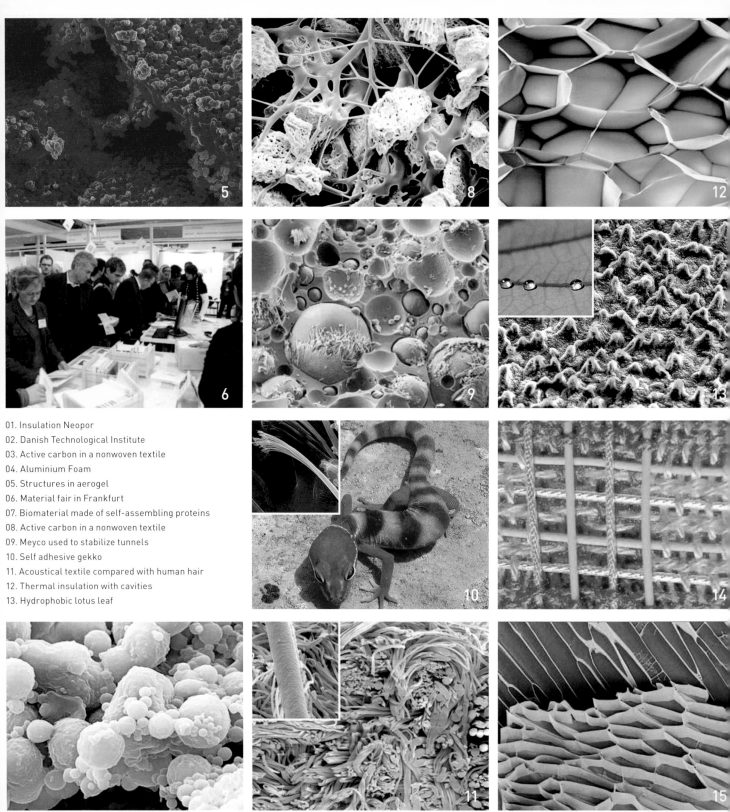

01. Insulation Neopor
02. Danish Technological Institute
03. Active carbon in a nonwoven textile
04. Aluminium Foam
05. Structures in aerogel
06. Material fair in Frankfurt
07. Biomaterial made of self-assembling proteins
08. Active carbon in a nonwoven textile
09. Meyco used to stabilize tunnels
10. Self adhesive gekko
11. Acoustical textile compared with human hair
12. Thermal insulation with cavities
13. Hydrophobic lotus leaf

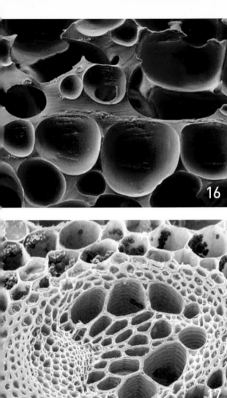

16

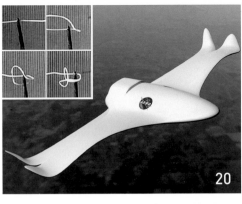

20

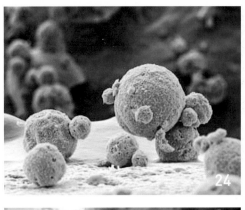

24

17

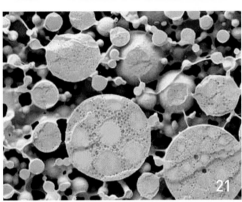

21

25

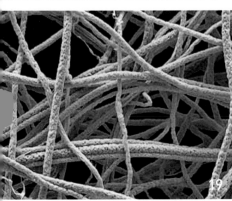

18

22

14. Textile with interwoven wires
15. High-performance stabilizer
16. Compression-resistant foam
17. Section of af plant stem
18. Ecosystems in coral reefs
19. Electrospun nanofibers
20. Shape memory materials
21. Environmentally automotive coating
22. Material fair in Frankfurt
23. Carbon nano tubes
24. Metal oxide particles from batteries
25. Cellular nano foam
26. Electrospinning

19

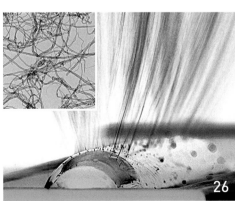

26

LAB IV

Things which necrose

Limited time-span, biodegradable pavilion + prototype.
A pavilion that disappears slowly, in accordance with its temporary status.

To achieve this necrosis or biodegradability we will develop a specific bioplastic from corn or sugar cane, which can be programmed with different life spans, depending on the following parameters:

– Chemical composition (natural substances without petrochemical ingredients) of the Bioplastic

– Thickness of the veins of the moulded panels that form the wall, floor, roof. Degradation over time is inversely proportionate to the thickness.

– Relationship between the degree of humidity and temperature. We will be able to control both these parameters by spraying wet vapour on the surfaces and on the top of the pavilion itself to increase or decrease the rate of degradation.

Scenario

1. Development of a bioplastic with hydrosoluble polymers from agricultural material.

2. Design of a panelling relief, integrating membrane and structure of the building, which can be strategically and slowly 'necrosed' by controlling the atmospheric humidity.

3. Development of an injection moulding system by means of CNC machine processing, 5 axes

4. Installation of mist nozzles as a dimmer system to emphasize or reduce the 'disappearing protocol'.

5. Regulation of the life span of a temporary building (in the first experiment on one floor) from its construction to its decomposition.

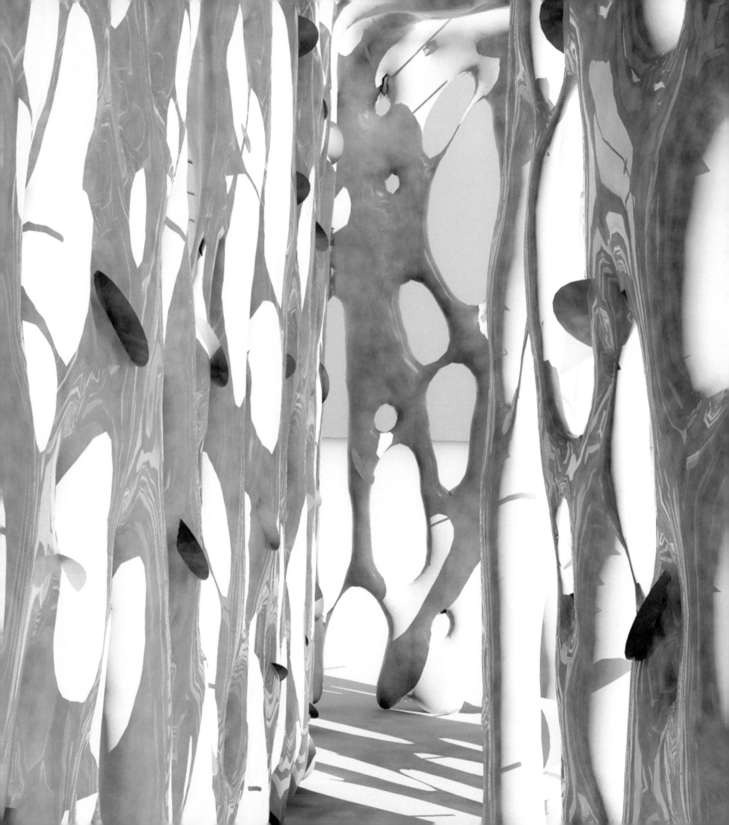

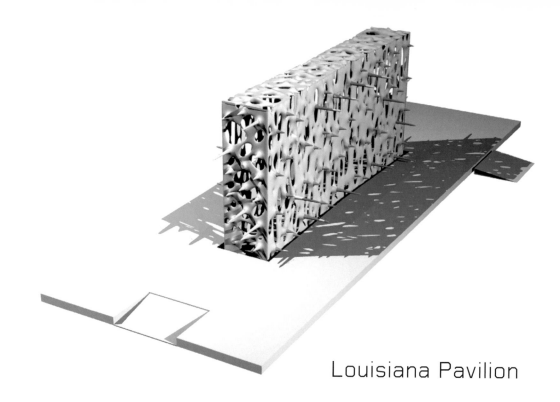

Louisiana Pavilion

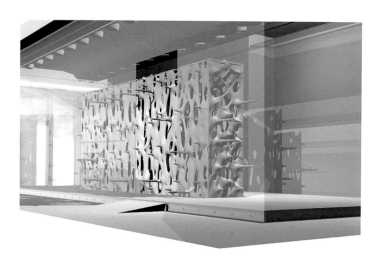

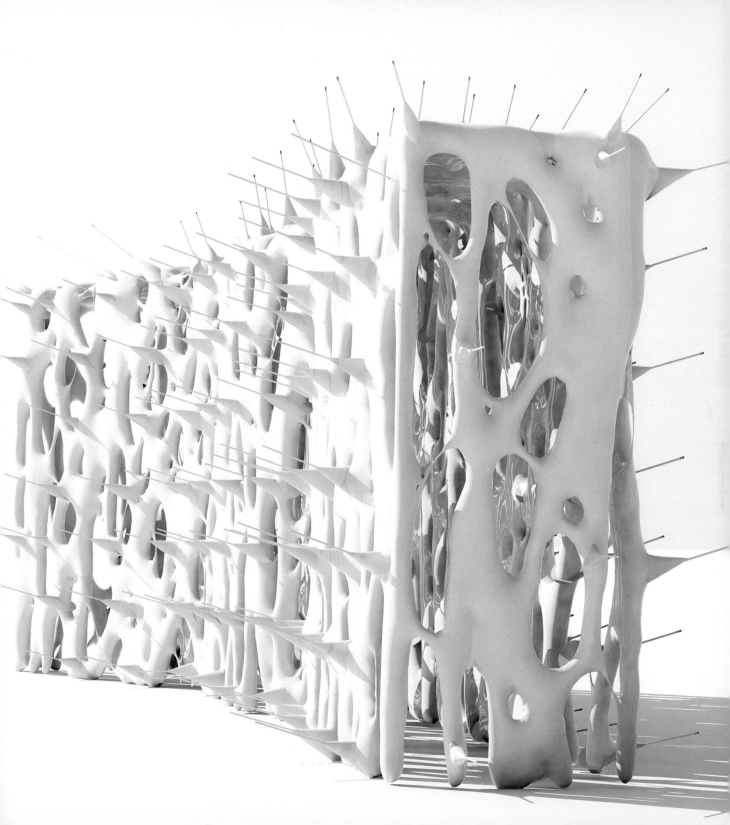

R&Sie(n)
Interview with
François Roche

By Michael Juul Holm

MJH: The exhibition you are participating in at the Louisiana is about the challenges posed to architecture by the changes in the climatic balance and the imbalances in our consumption of natural resources – in broad outline it's about sustainability. What are your feelings about that term? Can the projects for your office be seen at all as part of the wave of 'sustainability architecture'?

FR: We don't have anything against appearing in that context – of course not – and we would also like to contribute to the spectrum that is unrolling. But we never use the term sustainable. Since the beginning, almost twenty years ago, we have cared a lot about the narrative and the narrator, about the question of where is being spoken from. We've tried to look critically at the authorial voice that comes to expression in the work etc., and our approach has been to work in the field of uncertainty: to zoom in on the indeterminable, the ambiguous, what is in the fundamental sense interesting, that is what is 'in among things' (*inter esse* is Latin and literally means 'to be in among things' – ed.). We would like to use architecture to clarify connections as well as differences. Think about the two sides of a carpet. We would like to include both the intended pattern and the hidden weave of the underside. Sustainability is a matter of definitions and how far you go in your analysis. As far as our projects are concerned we haven't taken the analysis all the way through on that issue; in the first instance we focus on the task, on the problem, on the place – the field. Is it sustainable to have an oxe pull a cable connected to a cylinder that generates current for the hydraulic system that controls the facade of a building? I don't know. We did that sort of thing in Thailand. Or for example when we use electrostatically charged materials that collect some of the polluted by-products from the burning of fossil fuels in traffic, and improve the climate locally close to the building in question? I don't know if that can be described as 'sustainable', but it's certainly the intention to make certain intolerable conditions more tolerable – 'sustainable' in that sense. The specific case I'm thinking about is the future museum of art in Bangkok, which will have wires stretched across the outside of the building that sort of 'grow a fur' by attracting the carbon particles to them. What was a condition of life that is unavoidable for the local population will not only be remedied a little, but above all will be clarified and thematicized. One of the reasons for the quite unheard-of air pollution is the lack of public transportation. We would like to help to make that visible.

Why is it important to tell stories with architecture?
– Of course I don't mean fiction that simply lives in its own right. But each project speaks to us of something in particular, it tells a story in the sense that it articulates certain circumstances, typically certain factors in the existing milieu or the local culture. In Paris we've drawn up a project where a robot uses empty wine bottles from the return system in randomized construction that adds new spaces and surfaces to an existing building. That's a story about many things, among others a French type of addiction, about pleasure and abandonment – if there were no more wine bottles the project would come to a halt. That's unlikely to be the problem in Paris at the moment! But we wouldn't care either to be viewed as 'storytelling' architects in the modern management sense the word has taken on. We would probably – pretensions away – like to be understood as Situationists in the tradition of Guy Debord. That is, as people who are never completely naive, who are always a little suspicious and get their bearings from the circumstances of the mission itself – from who is being spoken to, who is speaking etc. – and thus let the basic structure of the narrative grow out of the urge to reveal something, to make something evident that would otherwise just further alienate people. That's so to speak the philosophical legacy of Situationism, and at the same time we have the action-oriented and concrete aspect of the word Situationist: We deal with the situation.

You call it a 'philosophical' legacy, but Situationism was first and foremost an artistic movement. And some of your projects resemble certain kinds of contemporary art – the kind that stresses the social responsibility of art and has its part to play in politics and society …
– We have close connections with artists, both personally and professionally. And as part of our basis I suppose we also have the idea of reversing the traditional roles and blurring the whole grand idea of authority and authorship. Artists have been involved in many of the things we've done, and I'm very inspired for example by the collaboration

between Claude Parent and Yves Klein on drawings of 'air architecture', dematerialized architecture. But we don't see ourselves as artists. We've been totally de-romanticized when it comes to that. We also work, among much else, with the staging (in a good sense) of confusion, making physical space and thus also mental space for the ambiguities. In this we are allied with the artists. People can't be certain whether what comes from here comes out of a purely architectural meaning-context or whether there are also other layers at play. We like to make buildings where the identity isn't so hard-and-fast, where the formative principle may for example be that the architecture is a part of the surroundings – grows out of the forest, to use one example. Dis-identifies itself, in a way, so you don't immediately recognize it as architecture.

Why all this blurring of identity and author?
– In fact it's a strategy for making something clearer. Architects are often closely connected with power, with political and economic power. It's important that they constantly question the source. Michel Foucault's discussion of who it is that is speaking, of the conditions of speech – we have to repeat that questioning for ourselves. By working consciously with artists in our projects we can shuffle the territories around a bit and open the door to a multiplicity of possible interpretations.

Let's talk a little about the laboratory you're presenting at the Louisiana. It's a temporary construction, a fragment and a test prototype for a much bigger project to be launched in Stockholm next year?
– Yes, what we're setting up here is a part of a building, a pavillon, that bears its own death within it, its own cessation. Earlier in the history of architecture people worked with temporary buildings, temporary installations, but they typically used modules and easily-dismantled elements or tents, inflatables a.o., that can be transported somewhere else. What's new here is that we work with materials that have time built in: in the course of the four months of the exhibition our little building will go through different phases on its way to its final dissolution. That's how it's programmed, created as it is from water-soluble polymers based on sugar and corn. The moisture in the room and in the pond in which the structure stands will slowly make the building decompose and melt; those who visit the

exhibition at an early stage will have quite a different experience from those who come a few weeks later. We see it as a test of what you could call a vanishing-protocol. It's the least safe of the Three Little Pigs' houses, the one the Big Bad Wolf would blow down first, and we find this exploration of lifetime and danger, risk, fragility etc. profoundly fascinating. Parts of the wall will disappear completely, while others will be left as rudimentary structures. It's also an attempt to understand time, the arrow of time as an irreversible fact. And it'll be exciting to see how it turns out. It's never been done with this technique before.

Interesting as philosophical show-and-tell teaching or as an artistic project ...
– But in fact it isn't just that. Construction methods like these may become hugely relevant quicker than we can imagine. Just think: there are island states like Tuvalu that are already less than one metre above sea level. In just a few decades they'll be gone, and today it's already forbidden to erect buildings there that can't be taken down and moved in their entirety to other places. Stockholm, for which the project is intended, is a city that lies in the middle of its archipelago. If the sea rises just half a metre it will have a significant effect on the topography of the city. Our building doesn't have to be taken down, it will disappear by itself and end up in the sea without leaving traces. That's complete dissolution, and the house will be eaten by the fishes. At the Louisiana too there will be fish in the pond that can eat the detritus into which the building decomposes.

That sounds like absolutely radical cradle-to-cradle thinking?
– Yes, it even rhymes a bit with it. Cradle to Cradle in the Biblical source: ashes to ashes, dust to dust. Without buying the whole mysticism Steiner developed in his Anthroposophical thinking, we're interested in the ideas of natural circulation he talks about. It fits very well with that philosophy that a building in fact completely disappears without leaving pollution in the process, and even gives nitrogen back to nature. But it's difficult to get to the bottom of the idea of the global footprint. Like everyone else we're interested in the new signs we see of a radical shift in the balance. I myself have been to Svalbard recently, for example,

and have spoken to experts who tell me that up to five per cent of the polar bears born today are hermaphrodites – is that a desperate genetic survival strategy, a Darwinistic lifeline, or is it just a sign of poisoning? I find it very difficult to establish the absolute certainty you need to decide on, or even just understand, these issues. We're all for science, so I hope this doesn't sound like obscurantism, but I do think there's a fundamental uncertainty that should be represented, right down to the aesthetic level. We like our projects to wear that uncertainty on their sleeve.

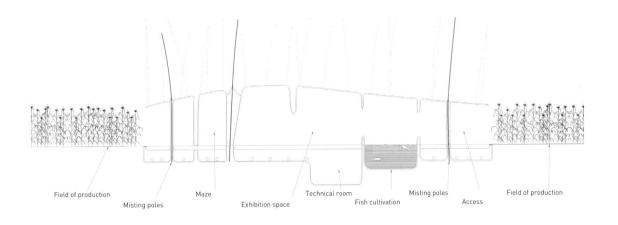

Field of production

Misting poles

Maze

Exhibition space

Technical room

Fish cultivation

Misting poles

Access

Field of production

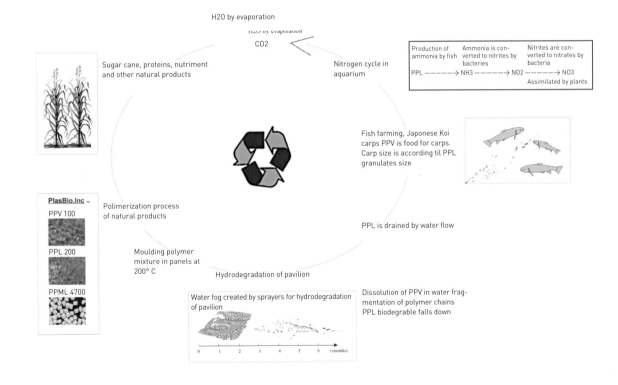

H2O by evaporation

H2O by evaporation

CO_2

Sugar cane, proteins, nutriment and other natural products

Nitrogen cycle in aquarium

Production of ammonia by fish	Ammonia is converted to nitrites by bacteries	Nitrites are converted to nitrates by bacteria
PPL ----→ NH3	----→ NO2	----→ NO3
		Assimilated by plants

Fish farming, Japonese Koi carps PPV is food for carps. Carp size is according til PPL granulates size

PlasBio.Inc
PPV 100

PPL 200

PPML 4700

Polimerization process of natural products

PPL is drained by water flow

Moulding polymer mixture in panels at 200° C

Hydrodegradation of pavilion

Water fog created by sprayers for hydrodegradation of pavilion

Dissolution of PPV in water fragmentation of polymer chains PPL biodegrable falls down

Stockholm Project

Climate Machine

Urban Agriculture in Berlin, Germany, 2007
Ton Matton

In various research projects Ton Matton seeks to achieve a synthesis of traditional rural life with a hypermodern lifestyle. He believes that growing fruit and vegetables and keeping livestock in urban spaces can function as a sort of social glue to bind culturally disparate communities together in socially healthy, positive ways. His Climate Machine is an optimistic research machine: it

encourages social healing in the city by turning public spaces into productive agricultural spaces. Grass areas are planted and cultivated as lawns; others are used to graze animals. Greenhouse lights, irrigation systems, and warm and cold air fans all provide suitable climates where flora and fauna can thrive. Ton Matton is introducing a parallel agricultural system to the urban context involving food production, participants from a wide range of backgrounds and the development of a new trading system.

Greeting to the Sun

Zadar coast promenade in Croatia, 2007
Nikola Basic

The city installation *Greeting to the Sun* on the Zadar coast promenade is motivated by the use of high technology in the design of new places in the city – urban areas with a strong spatial and symbolic character.

Light energy from the sun is transformed into electrical energy to create light experiences after sunset. The primary role of the installation is to facilitate physical and symbolic communication with the sun, but its practical result is the production of electrical energy to light up the whole coast promenade.

The play of light comes from three different programmes. The first programme connects with the sound of a sea organ transposed into sporadic images on the surface of the sun circle. The second programme is based on the interaction between the installation and passers-by. When they step into the sun circle it is registered by a sensor that initiates a special light effect. These effects are sporadic and varied, so that it looks as though each individual pedestrian triggers an individual light effect. Several pedestrians and the dynamics of their movements create unpredictable images from cumulative individual light impulses. The third programme is based on the video artist's thematic use of lighting design, as experienced through the new easily-understood technology. *Greeting to the Sun* invites both artists and passers-by to form their ideas in cooperation with nature, or simply to satisfy a primitive human urge to play that has been an underlying element in every culture.

Clouds
An Te Liu

Cloud, 2008
An Te Liu

Site-specific installation for the 11th International Architecture Exhibition of the Venice Biennale.

Cloud consists of domestic air purification appliances produced and consumed around the world over the last decade. They wash, filter, ionize, ozonize and sterilize the air around us, shielding us from bacteria, allergens, germs, spores, dust and other harmful things. Armada-like clusters converge to create a floating polis, perhaps a city of the future, but they also recall past visions of the future.

With Cloud An Te Liu has taken modernism's rhetoric of purity and hygiene to a point where the idea of the traditional shelter has dissolved into completely controlled environment-bubbles, where all the needs of humanity are met by technological systems and devices – everything is absolutely clean.

Photo Stefano Graziani © La Biennale di Venezia

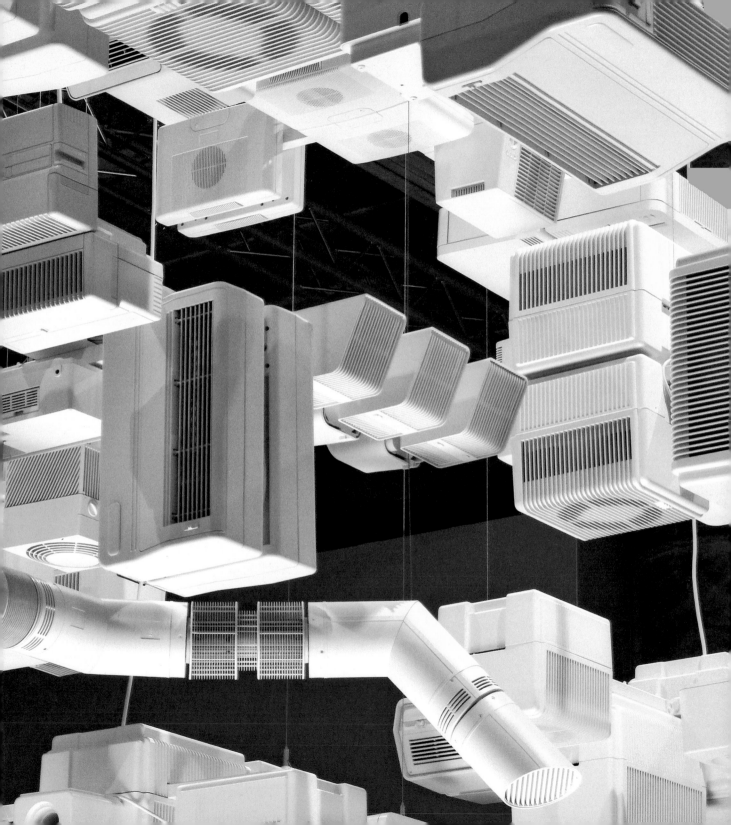

FRONTIERS OF ARCHITECTURE II
Green Architecture for the Future

Edited by Michael Juul Holm & Kjeld Kjeldsen
Assisted by Mette Marie Kallehauge & Jeanne Rank

© 2009 Louisiana Museum of Modern Art and the contributors
All works reproduced by agreement with the contributors and kind permission of the copyright holders

Design Steen Heide, Henrik Obel
Cover illustration by R&Sie(n), from the project Olzweg (p.110)
Translations by James Manley
Technical consultants Monica Lauster, Erik Olsen
Print Rosendahls
ISBN 978-87-91607-70-7
Printed in Denmark 2009

This catalogue was published on the occasion of the exhibition
FRONTIERS OF ARCHITECTURE II
Green Architecture for the Future

Credits for the exhibition on page 2

Photo: © Imageselect (8-9), © Ecosistema Urbano (10-17, 22), © Schrumpfende Städte // Shrinking Cities, Büro Philipp Oswalt (20-21), © Photo: Herb Lingl/aerialarchives.com (21), © Saori Kawashita (21), © Regionalverband Ruhr, Essen (21), © Ecosistema Urbano, Emilio P. Doiztua + Roland Halbe (23), © Boeri Studio (24), © Boeri Studio, Silva (25), © Rogers Stirk Harbour + Partners (26), © MVRDV (27), © Ton Venhoeven, Copijn (28), © Patrick Blanc (29), Patrick Blanc with SANAA: 21th Century Museum of Contemporary Art in Kanasawa, Japan (29), © T.R. Hamzah & Yeang Sdn. Bhd, © LLewelyn Davies Yeang (30), © William McDonough + Partners (31, 102-107), © R&Sie(n) (32-33, 100-101, 110-111, 127-128, 133-135), © Tanja Jordan Arkitekter / Konsulent, Kirsten Birk, arkitekt maa / COWI (34-35), © Lacaton & Vassal (36-37), © Fréderic Druot Architecture (38-39), © COBE (40), © Entasis (41), © Instituto Jaime Lerner (42-43), © Michel Desvigne (44-45), © Foster + Partners (46-55), © NASA (64-65), © Sauerbruch Hutton (66-67), © Mario Cucinella Architects, Daniele Domenicali (68-69, 83), © Transsolar/ockertundpartner (70-71), © Solomon Cordwell Buenz, Chicago, USA (72), © Kuwabara Payne Mckenna Blumberg Architects KPMB, Toronto, Canada (73), © Behnisch, Behnisch & Partner now Behnisch Architekten, Stuttgart, Germany (74), © Behnish Architekten, Stuttgart, Germany (75, 77), © Steven Holl Architects, New York, USA (photo: Iwan Baan) (76), © Atelier Lion: Claire PIGUET (77), © Mette Lange Architects (80), © photo: Kurt Hörbst (81), © Andreas Trier Mørch/arkitekturbilleder.dk (82), © PTW Architects (84), © Studio Monte Rosa, 8093 Zürich / Bearth & Deplazes Architekten AG, 7000 Chur (85), © Philippe Rahm Architects (86-93), © 1965 François Dallegret / ADAGP (Paris) 2001 (94-99), © United_Bottle by United_Bottle Group UBG (Dirk Hebel, Tobias Klauser, Hanspeter Logo, Jörg Stollmann) (108-109), © Takanobu Sakuma and Paper Log House Turkey (112 ø), © Shigeru Ban Architects (112 n), © Kartikeya Shodhan, (113), © GrAT – Gruppe Angepasste Technologie (Center for Appropriate Technology) (114-115), © Sarah Wigglesworth Architects (116-117), © 3XN (118-124), © MattonOffice, Ton Matton & Björn Ortfeld (136-137), © Nikola Basic / Stipe Surac (138-139), © Cameraphoto Arte / La Biennale di Venezia (140), © La Biennale di Venezia (141).

125-127: All electron microscopic is from; BASF the chemical company. Other photos is from; Danish Technological Institute, Elmarco, North Carolina State University - Collage of Textiles, Mya Breitbart – University of South Florida, and Nasa Research Center

Realdania
Sponsor of architectural exhibitions at Louisiana